I AM HAPPY

How to go from being a 'HAPPY MESS'

to finding true HAPPINESS

By Elena Vasilenka

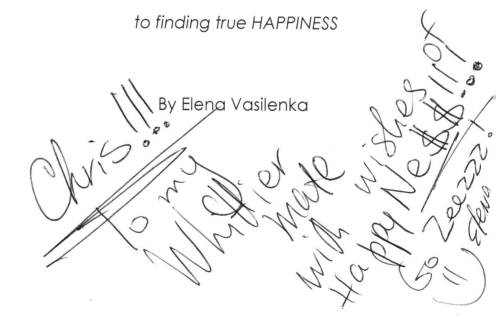

www.7-publishing.com

ISBN-13: 978-1540431455
ISBN-10: 1540431452

Cover Photo: Jerry Zalez

Disclaimer: Always consult your physician before beginning this or any other exercise program. Nothing in this book is to be construed as medical advice. The benefits attributed to the practice of Naam Yoga Therapies come from the centuries - old yogic tradition. Results will vary with individuals.

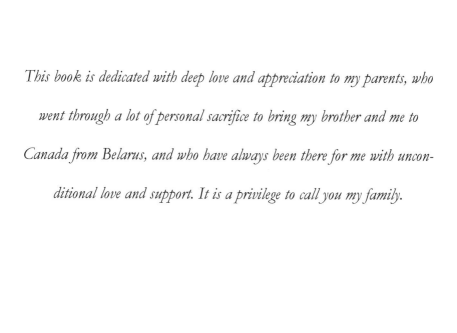

This book is dedicated with deep love and appreciation to my parents, who went through a lot of personal sacrifice to bring my brother and me to Canada from Belarus, and who have always been there for me with unconditional love and support. It is a privilege to call you my family.

CONTENTS

PART 2

ACKNOWLEDGEMENTS

My boundless love and gratitude to my Spiritual Teacher, Dr. Joseph Michael Levry, the founder of Naam Yoga, for teaching me this invaluable yogic technology and for having most unconditional and unshakable faith in me, my true potential and in the possibility of my healing. I am forever grateful and honored to be your student.

With gratitude in my heart I want to thank my best friends, Peter Glebo and John Do who have always been there for me in my most darkest moments; Tommy Tune for being my role model and a constant source of inspiration; my mentor Therese Walsh for believing in me and my message; my brother Sergey Vasilenka and my beloved friends Sunniva Maguire, Eugiene Jonathan Pisarevsky, Dr. Maria Manzanares, William Leamon, Amanda Plant, Courtney Miller, Nicole Evans, Woopy Enright, Dienna D'Olimpio, Jenn Kennedy, Rowenna and Megan Chaskey, Malissa Young, Bisila Bokoko; to my editors, Anna Hurtgen and Dr. Caren Rich; my friend and a best-selling author Sean Gardner for introducing me to my incredible publisher, Saba Tekle, whose encouragement made this book happen with such an ease, plus many others for their assistance, love, input and support.

PREFACE

Thank you for reading this book with an open heart and mind and for giving me a chance to share my story of the profound transformation that happened in my life in just a few short years. The life that I now joyfully call my own is inspired by the powerful teachings of Dr. Joseph Michael Levry, founder of Naam Yoga, and a world-renowned mystic, musician, yogi and Master of Universal Kabbalah. I am forever grateful to Dr. Levry for teaching me Naam Yoga and Divine Spiritual Wisdom, and for showing me how to get in touch with the teacher that dwells inside of my own heart. During my years of practice with this extraordinary spiritual technology, I went from being an entirely unhappy, miserable person, with many mental, physical and emotional challenges to being the most positive, happy person that I ever imagined I could be. Sometimes people ask me why I am always so happy and smiling all of the time, regardless of what is going on in my life. Some even regard me as "the most positive and happy person they have ever met." Although I am humbled and grateful to be called that, it was not always the case. It was quite the opposite actually! It is with much gratitude for Dr. Levry, for the teachings of Naam Yoga and for all of the people who touched my heart throughout the most intense and profound years of personal healing, that I am sharing my story with you. I hope that my journey will inspire you to create the same or even bigger transformations in your own life so that you as well can live your best, happiest and healthiest life ever. I wish you to be truly happy and in love with yourself, others and your life.

PART 1

CHAPTER 1

New York City and Me - The Way We Used to Be

> *"Hello, I love you. Won't you tell me your name? People are strange when you're a stranger. Faces look ugly when you're alone." ~ Jim Morrison*

Welcome to my world. My name is Elena. Or is it Alyona, or Alex? You see, they are all my names. Elena is Russian. Alyona is Belorussian and Alex is my middle name. I am not sure what to call myself. I feel strange, alone and convinced that I am ugly or at least fat. Probably both. For sure, I am unlovable and nothing good will ever come out of me. It is 2010 and I am twenty-eight years old. I live in Manhattan in a gorgeous apartment overlooking Union Square. I am in a relationship with a great guy, Tom, who could be the love of my life, if I only knew how to love. Don't get me wrong. I have been in love before. At ten years old I fell in love with bananas — deep, passionate, eleven-bananas-a-day-if-you-don't-stop-me, kind of love. You see, my mother and grandmother fought all of the time when I was little. After one of those fights my mother told her that she was not allowed to see me anymore. As we were very close, I was devastated. One day my grandmother sneaked into my school and brought me one perfectly yellow, beautiful, delicious banana, hugged me, and ran out. From that day forward, every time I was sad, I would eat a banana and feel better instantly. That confirmed my status as an emotional eater and started my lifelong love affair with this magical yellow fruit. I'm pretty sure that it's not the love you're supposed to feel for your partner, or even more so for yourself, but it felt real to me.

Back to Tom. Tom happens to be tall, kind, smart, handsome and a multi-millionaire. Yep, every girl's dream guy to be with. I am a model. I am size four and super toned. I was once sent on a casting to the head office of Victoria Secret, a real enchanted place, every guy's dream place to visit. I was excited and nervous at the same time, thinking that anyone who walked in there would have to look like a Victoria Secret Angel just to be allowed to enter. I was relieved when they let me go through the door. Still, once I got inside they told me I was too fat, or too "big", to be exact. It's okay, I thought to myself, I can lose more weight. Moreover, I told myself, they are right, I am too fat. What was I even thinking going to a Victoria Secret casting?

Yes, my mind works like that most of the time. Negative and mean words towards myself are the ones I hear in my mind most of the time. With all of this negative mental chatter and anger toward myself and the world taking a lot of my energy, I am blissfully unaware of the fact that very soon my life of ease and luxury will completely disappear. The days of not fitting into size two Victoria Secret jeans would be the least of my problems. For now I have no idea that I will be sent on a journey of humbleness, self-forgiveness and self-healing. I cannot even imagine that anything in my life could be remotely different in any way, the bad parts or the good.

My best friends are celebrities and talented artists, all amazing and loving beings who care for me and are fun to be around. They tell me I am beautiful all of the time. I secretly think they are crazy, that they have had too much champagne, and I just smile politely when they say it. Why are they so nice to me anyway? I am never okay with it. I wish they were a bit meaner and abusive so that I could relax and be in my element around them. Nevertheless, I love them in any case, and maybe one day I finally will get used to their sweetness. Besides, no matter how many times they say that I am pretty and take another beautiful (so they say) photo of me, deep down I know the truth — that I am fat and unattractive. I think that maybe I should try to be funny so that people would like me more. Or maybe it would be helpful to buy people things and pay for their drinks when we go out. That is a big secret to making people like you more. I think I read that it in "How to Win Friends and Influence People." Great book. Okay, that is a joke. I did not read that there, but I think it works. People seem to want to hang out with you when you are footing the bills. Another thing that I tell myself is — only say what people want to hear. Never, ever argue Elena. Keep your anger inside. Bottle it up. You need friends.

What else shall I tell you about my life? In winter, Tom and I go on vacations to Turks and Caicos, St. Barts and to West Palm Beach, Florida. In summer, we rent a house with our friends in the Hamptons. There is something very special about eating a $40 salad next to one of The Real Housewives of New York City that keeps us going back there repeatedly. On Sundays, when Tom and I are in New York City, we usually go to the "Church of Saks Fifth Avenue". I saved him, you see. Before we met, he was going to "North Face", but I showed him the light. We are both very committed to our church and to the worship of our lords: Valentino, Louis, and Armani. We are so devoted that we once went there during Tom's best friend's wedding. Thankfully the church they were getting married in, St. Patrick's Cathedral, was conveniently located right next to ours and so we went shopping right after the vows. While everyone else was getting drunk at the bar and waiting for the bride and groom to arrive at the Yale Club, we were praying. I was praying that I could still fit into a size four dress (sitting through a church ceremony can easily make anyone gain at least two pounds!) and Tom was praying that I would not spend too much on his Amex card. Yes, it took him a while to come around to the understanding of the "Divine Truth", which is that the more you give back to the spiritual source that opens your heart and fills it with joy, the more blessings will come into your life. It is a cosmic law, and there is nothing you can do about it. Give and you shall receive. I read it in my Bible - Cosmopolitan magazine that is. Now come to think about it, I am pretty sure it was a chapter on hot and steamy make-out sessions, but you should always read between the lines and see the higher meaning of any spiritual scripture or magazine. Naturally, being the giver that I am, I was giving Tom more and more clothes to try on, as we were, after all, attempting to be productive and get back to the wedding dinner. As Tom was trying his next $2,000 suit on, I felt so relieved that he had finally started to believe in Armani. Everyone knows that it is hard to build a life with someone who does not share the same values with you. What is nice about our "church" is that most of our friends go there as well. It is a beautiful place to reconnect with your outer self, with your community and to share something meaningful, something higher than your small mortal self. One day I will be gone, but Chanel is forever. My faith in Chanel and other higher powers of luxury gives me strength to face each day with confidence. When I leave my house and have on less than $10,000 worth of clothing and accessories, I feel like I am not worthy of love and attention, that I am not good enough, and all I really want is to be "good enough".

I want people to value me and like me and that is why I go to the "church". It is in it that I finally got my self-esteem back. It was cruelly taken away from me at the age of three. The boy I had a crush on in kindergarten pulled away my blanket at nap time and saw my underwear, which happened to be white with orange and black stripes. He laughed so hard and called me "tiger" for the rest of kindergarten. He never fell in love with me. I am sure it would have been different if I had been wearing pretty underwear that day — perhaps blue with flowers or maybe pink ones with cute little hearts. But tiger stripes? Thanks mom for dressing me in those ridiculous panties that cost me my first failed relationship! I never told her about that embarrassing moment, but I wish she knew how traumatized I was. Well, look who's laughing now you mean little boy! I am now fully accepted and loved by my sophisticated New York City friends, thanks to my strong faith in haute couture and Tom's bottomless Amex card.

Along with my superior faith, I am very much into a healthy lifestyle and I love everything organic. My dear friends Tommy Tune, Peter Glebo and John Do once threw me a surprise birthday party where everything was organic, even the Veuve Clicquot champagne. I know this because each item had an organic sticker on it, the ones that you see on bananas. I later learned that Peter's friend put the stickers on everything herself. Anyway, as you can see, I am very serious about my organic lifestyle. I only buy my groceries at Whole Foods. I assume that if something is more expensive then it has to be of better quality, so I always buy the most expensive brands available. Besides, cheaper brands are always on the bottom shelf and I am not bending down just to save a few dollars as I am six feet tall with my high heels on, and my legs are too sore after working out with my trainer. That's right, I have a personal trainer on top of my extravagant gym membership. The condo we live in has a gym of its own, but I definitely need the second one, as they treat me very nice there. They know my name by heart at the fifteen-dollar-a-drink juice bar. I also go to an elite yoga studio, even though they offer yoga classes at my overpriced fancy gym as well as at my condo. I like paying the extra $20 per class. It makes me value it more and I try harder at my 'utkavaasana' or whatever it is called. Like a true New Yorker, or at least like every girl who pretends she is on a virtual set of "Sex and the

City", I always wear high heels and take a cab everywhere I go. I abhor the subway; it is loud, hot, confusing and God forbid, might take me to Brooklyn by mistake. When I go out for cocktails with my friends, I often suggest the Four Seasons Hotel bar. When my girlfriends complain about its $25 Cosmopolitans or how expensive Manhattan is in general, I smile politely, but in my mind I can see that they clearly do not belong in Manhattan. No complaints about my beloved Manhattan, not in front of me! Moreover, Manhattan is not even expensive. They are just crybabies who need to get it together. (Yes, I love judging others and seeing what is wrong with them — so much fun!) Seriously, why would anyone want to pay less than $25 for a Cosmopolitan anyway? It might be made with cheap vodka then and I am pretty sure that cheap vodka is bad for your health and causes wrinkles. I choose organic vodka anytime I am out, knowing that I am doing my body good.

We have a housekeeper, so I never have to clean or do laundry. It is my favorite thing to do — not clean. I once read in an interview with Julia Roberts that she cleans her own house and that she is not beneath cleaning her own toilet bowl. That's just crazy talk! I am not only too good to clean; I am also terrible at it. I like to create jobs, you see. I am an entrepreneur of sorts and by having a housekeeper, I can proudly contribute to the American economy.

If you were to take a peek at my life from the outside, you would probably find me at a fancy polo party in the Hamptons, champagne glass in hand, the embodiment of the picture perfect "trophy wife". You would say, "Wow, her life is perfect. She has it all." Welcome to my perfect illusion.

CHAPTER 2

A Sweet Happy Mess: Made in the USSR

"Happiness is a mental or emotional state of well-being characterized by positive or pleasant emotions ranging from contentment to intense joy." ~ *Wikipedia.*

"Happy Mess is a mentally and emotionally unstable girl living in New York City, eating ice cream under the covers for breakfast, picking her face at night; highly volatile, negative, pessimistic in her thinking, and appearing completely normal and happy to the rest of the world." ~ *Elenapedia*

With my life being so picture perfect, you might ask, why am I so confused and unhappy? Why am I so tough on myself? Why do I tell myself that I am fat and ugly when clearly I am not? Perhaps you should know that aside from all of the glitz and glamour, I am negative, pessimistic, self-destructive and severely depressed. I was officially diagnosed at the age of twenty with manic depression and bipolar disorder. I am not sure if my doctor exaggerated it, or if I really was that messed up, but I felt awful and depressed for as long as I could remember myself and I thought of ending my life on several occasions. These days I am doing much better. I am not suicidal anymore and that is a huge progress, however, I do think that my life and everything in it sucks. Ok, maybe not everything. Manhattan is awesome and my friends are super fabulous. But Tom sucks, his friends suck, his family sucks, my family sucks and I definitely suck — big time. I do not just dislike myself — I pretty much hate myself. I am just not fully aware of it. I am severely addicted to sugar and coffee. I drink coffee all of the time, even though it makes me shaky and nervous, and I read that it is full of chemicals and is dangerous for the system (unless shade-grown). I will eat anything sweet in front of me as long as nobody is watching.

I am from Belarus, a former Soviet Block country. It is a place where people have very little and work very hard. Possibilities and opportunities in life are very limited. Looking back on it, everyone shared a collective "oppression" and "life is hard" mentality. The general approach to raising children was not very encouraging. When I was born, the doctor told my mother to only feed me three times a day, at set times, and ignore me completely should I cry in between. She was only eighteen years old and thought this was the right way to do things — to go by the book, by some doctor's rules. When she was not around and I would cry with hunger, my grandma would soak white bread in water and give it to me to suck on in a cloth. She did not know that the simple carbohydrates in white bread have the same chemical effect on the body as sugar. She was creating the 'sugar equals happiness' connection in her granddaughter from her first days on this planet and thus ruining all of her chances to become a Victoria Secret Angel. From age five or so I could eat the whole box of cookies or candies at once, if you did not stop me. My binge eating went so out of hand over the years, that I decided to enroll to a nutrition institute in NYC to become a Holistic Health Coach. My plan is to help others overcome eating disorders and depression through healing the body with food. That way I will be so busy helping others that I will have no time to pay attention to my own misery. Plus, my future clients will never be able to tell that I have any food issues thanks to my trainer, my gym memberships and my fake but very believable happy attitude. But where were we? Oh yes, back to the story of how I became a sugar addict. Now you can see that I have even more reasons to blame my mother for ruining my life by starving me and turning me into a carb addict. By the time I was sent to live with my grandparents at the age of six in what is now another country (back then it was all one big Soviet Union), so that I could go to a better school, I was well on my way to becoming a mess. My dad was in the Red Army and shortly after my birth we moved to a small military base in a middle of a deep forest in Russia where there were no schools. The closest one was in a small village forty minutes away by bus. My parents had good intentions. Wanting me to grow up educated and "well-rounded," they sent a six-year-old Elena to Minsk, a city of one million people, to study and play tennis. In my mind, however, I decided that they simply did not like me that much, and so "tennis" or "better life" were key words indicating an excuse to get rid of me. It didn't help that I would only see them once a year, and I would have to travel alone on a train overnight from Minsk to Moscow in order to do so. I was six! What if I got the stations mixed up and got out in the wrong city? What would they do? There were no cell phones and I had no microchip on me that you could track me with like a lost pet. I was convinced that it would make no difference to them if I became misplaced. I wondered if I would have to use my grandparents' last name now that I was living with them and start calling them Mother and Father. I missed my parents and I could not really understand or express it back then. The only way to cope with it was to drink. Just kidding! I am from Belarus, but generally even we start a bit later than that. I did have an accidental encounter with vodka at the age of eleven when I drank what I thought was a bottle of water that my grandmother usually kept on her bedside table. That night, because I was sick, she had vodka in the bottle instead, to wipe my body down from a fever. Thankfully, drinking vodka was not a habit that stayed with me! My drug of choice was sugar, as you know by now. My grandmother had to hide anything sweet from me on a particular shelf she had all the way up by the ceiling. I was always plotting how to reach it when she was not around.

Now at twenty-eight, with twenty-two plus years of professional binge eating behind me, I often go to a grocery store after Tom falls asleep and buy ice-cream and cheesecake and stuff myself in front of the TV. I repeat this process in the morning after he goes to work. Now that I am with Tom I can afford to binge on expensive, premium organic treats, so I am super-selective. My indulgences are always "healthy"; it's a must! When I was young and penniless, my standards were different and I would eat anything in site. In college, there was a girl in my dorm who always kept her door unlocked. I knew exactly where she kept her Luna power bars and when she was not around, I would sneak into her room and eat a few of them. I am sure she had no idea who or what was helping her to finish another box of bars so fast, but she never locked her room. Yes, I stole sweets in my teenage years a lot. Sweets were a powerful drug for me, so much that even though I knew that stealing was bad, I could not help myself. I used to eat all of the Hershey Kisses that my college roommate kept in a bowl on her desk. I tried to explain to her that I could not stop, but it just reinforced in her mind that her foreigner roommate was an actual alien and she kept refilling the bowl hoping that one day I would get sick of them. That never happened. It was a private college and most of the kids there had a lot of money. I was on a scholarship and a work-study program. Therefore, I decided that an ice cream counter job on campus would be a match made in heaven for me, as I could eat unlimited ice cream in between shifts. I was on the Whittier College tennis team and constantly worked out so I was very fit. If you saw me, it was completely impossible to think that I could have a binge eating disorder that was so serious that I often contemplated ending my life. I did not know how to stop binging. I felt so utterly hopeless. I didn't think that I would ever find a cure.

CHAPTER 3

My Canadian "Roots"

At nineteen, before I ever even dreamed of living in the city that never sleeps, I moved to Toronto and my disorder got completely out of hand. I knew I had to do something about it or I wouldn't make it out alive. I decided to "cure" my addiction by asking a friend to keep my wallet in his house at all times, and to only take me to the grocery store once a week to buy some basic groceries. I thought that this would help me not to spend my entire paycheck on sweets and carbs. Little did I know that instead of fixing things, I would get myself into an even deeper trouble. I fell back into my college ways of stealing ice cream and candies, only now from grocery stores. One time when I couldn't fall asleep without any sugar in my system, and with only my driver license on me, I got dressed up and went to a corner store and tried to persuade the store clerk to buy my license in exchange for some ice cream. I told him that he could make a hefty profit from it by selling it to an underage girl who looked like me. I am sure that I looked and sounded crazy. He told me to get the heck out of there. Another night, still not being able to fall asleep without my fix, I went to a twenty-four hour restaurant at 3 AM. I ordered a huge slice of cake to eat and then I was planning to sit there until I could phone my friend later in the morning to bring my wallet. Luckily, after watching me sit there for hours, someone took pity on me (I said that I forgot my wallet at home) and paid the bill. Honestly, I did not mind sitting there all night, for as long as I could have my sugar, I was happy. I was acting like a junky and I realized that it was only a matter of time before I would end up being arrested for shoplifting. I could see the picture of me stuffing myself with ice cream, posted on the front door of every grocery store saying, "Do not admit!" I could not afford for my reputation to be ruined. Binging was my undercover, in the closet, when nobody's watching, kind of activity. None of my friends really knew how deeply troubled I was or that I always felt like my only real friend was sugar. Well, hardly anyone. After I realized I couldn't give my wallet away and not have any money on me ever, I decided to hire one of my unemployed friends. I told him that his new job would be to walk with me everywhere I went during the day, and to not allow me to buy anything sweet. He had strict orders not to listen to me when I would yell at him and tell him to go to hell. When he accepted the position, it was fun for about two hours. I was doing great. I was getting through my morning and I did not have any sweets. By the end of the day I wanted to kill him. Every time I wanted to stop by a store or a coffee shop and get my "fix," he would do his "job" and I would go into a rage, complete with insults and punching. I could not go a whole day without sugar and neither he nor anyone else could stay in my way. I fired him immediately.

The next week, I decided to try another genius solution, or so it seemed to me at the time. I maxed out my credit card to go to a $1000 per day holistic spa outside of Toronto for five days. It was the only place I could find at the time that offered a sugar detox program that I could get to in just a few hours and start cleansing my system, drinking clay, dirt, blended grass or whatever else they planned to give me. I was ready. I couldn't take it any longer. I was there for five days, extremely hungry and feeling like a huge fake, pretending that I belonged amongst the millionaire housewives who were there for some rest and relaxation. I felt so guilty and mad at myself for doing something so extravagant and spending all of my money, but I just didn't know how else to help myself. At the end of five days, I was five pounds thinner and completely broke. Ok, maybe the five pounds was worth it, I thought on the way back to Toronto. As soon as I got off of that bus and finished the last carrot they had given me to gently reintroduce solid foods into my system,

I headed straight to Starbucks and ordered a coffee, a muffin and a cheesecake slice to go. A few nights later, during another uncontrollable binge, I called my Mother and asked her to come and get me from my downtown apartment because I wanted to kill myself after I had finished eating my last serving of ice cream. That was my lowest point. I never went that far after that night again, but I kept binging and running away to juicing and detox places for years in hopes of putting an end to my cravings. After each detox program, I would head straight back to my coffee, muffins and cheesecakes. I thank God that I always had a good job that could support that dysfunctional lifestyle and bought me some time before I was ready for the real healing to happen.

One night my hairdresser invited me to a party in a popular downtown Toronto bar called "Pravda", which means "truth" in Russian. I find it to be a very interesting coincidence, since that was the night that I met Tom and my journey of discovering even greater truths began. Tom and I started to date and a year later he asked me to move with him to New York. I left my job to go and live with him. My detox spa trips went from being five days long to five weeks long and now in fancy places like West Palm Beach and the Hamptons. He was very supportive of my healing journey and, in fact, his first-year anniversary gift to me was to one of those spas. He really wanted me to get better. Detoxing in style at elite resorts and then coming back to binge on limitless amounts of sugar in New York City became a norm for me. I had no idea how to heal my eating disorder. I was just hoping that by staying away from sugar long enough at those spas one day I would finally change my pattern. But the only thing it changed was Tom's monthly credit card statements and I would feel just as miserable as I did before I left. Once I moved in with Tom, he had to make some changes in his life-style, as I asked him not to keep any sweets in the house, otherwise I would eat them all in one take. He had to keep his snacks and energy bars at his work. Despite all of this, nothing was changing inside of me. I was so desperate to heal so that I could be normal like Tom's friends' wives. I had no idea how to do it.

Here is another lovely detail for you about my fabulous "every girl's dream" kind of life. I pretend to be this perfect, happy, stylish NYC girl on the outside, yet feel so lonely and insecure about myself, my future and my purpose in life on the inside. On top of overeating sugar and over-caffeinating myself on a daily basis, I sometimes spend up to an hour a day in the bathroom picking at my skin. This form of Obsessive Compulsive Disorder is called dermatillomania and medical doctors claim that there is no cure for it. I had it since I was very young. Someone close to me once told me that I had bad skin and that my pores were clogged. I believed him and developed a major complex about my skin. Ever since then I have to make sure that every pore is completely cleaned. I often pick when I am nervous or upset about something. This activity calms me so much that I almost feel like I am in a trance while doing it. I especially love doing it the night before a photo shoot, which I will, for sure, cancel the next morning, because I am going to look terrible. I will spend the entire day hating myself for what I did to my face the night before, thinking what a loser I am and that I will never be successful in modeling with all my issues. My face is so full of scars that I never leave my house without makeup, even to the gym. During one of my "picking" sessions, I hurt my skin so badly that I was embarrassed to even go to a sauna in my building, as the front desk girl would see me without makeup afterward and I could not stand anyone seeing my face like that. I always try to pick my skin when Tom is asleep because he gets mad at me and tells me to stop. Even though I try to hide it, he can see my face the next day and he gets very upset. While he doesn't understand why I cannot control myself, he tries to be as compassionate as possible. Once he took all of the light bulbs out of the bathroom except for one, in hopes that I would not pick my face in the dark. I still did it. Eventually he had to put the lights back in order to shave and shower. I never realized how bad it was getting until my friend

Peter took me aside one morning during a trip to Province Town and asked me if I was on crystal meth. I was shocked that he would say something like that. He was one of my best friends and knew that I didn't do drugs. I was even more shocked when he asked if I had seen my face lately. His exact words were: "I am very concerned about you." I was shaken up about the reality of how serious my problem actually was, but still I could not stop.

When I feel happy and things are going well, I think that something is actually wrong with me. Naturally I find various ways to create drama in my life so that I will feel more normal. I create issues to fight about with my loved ones, find different things to be upset about and for sure there are many people in my life that I can blame, judge and criticize for all of this drama. You probably know by now that I do not really like my parents, I blame them for all my troubles and, in fact, I think they are the main cause of my depression and misery. I am constantly pissed off at Tom's relationship with his Mom. I think those two should be officially married, considering how they are super close with each other. I am angry with them most of the time. I actually enjoy being mad at them, as it provides me with a great topic of discussion with my friends. I am so good at suppressing my real feelings and anger that Tom doesn't even understand why I seem so unhappy all of the time. He likes to cheer me up by showing me videos of people who have been in a car accident or born with some physical limitation and still are able to have a positive attitude. He tells me that I have nothing to be upset about and that I should be grateful. I want to hit him with a frying pan for telling me how to feel and for using that "G" word in front of me. I am really not sure what it means, to be grateful. It is something foreign to me, I don't even know how it feels to feel that, and I think that the life that I have is normal and nothing special and so why would I ever be grateful for it?

I cannot stand people who seem really happy, and I am very jealous of them. Every morning during my coffee, muffin and ice cream breakfast, I watch "Regis and Kelly". Kelly makes me so mad. Why is she is so bubbly and happy? It must be nice to be her. She probably had a beautiful childhood where no one yelled at her, beat her up, told her how fat she was or how horrible her skin looked and that no one would ever marry her. I am so never going to be like her. I wish I could be like her, but I can't. Too much bad stuff has happened to me. I know that I am not born to be happy, rather destined to lead a miserable life of pain, anger and suffering. At least I will make sure that I am doing a good job of it. Would you like some more ice cream? Yes, please!

As you can tell by now, I have a lot going on in my brain and my emotional state is driving me bonkers. Yet somehow I manage to look and sound like one of those perfectly happy and "together" people when you meet me. I smile a big smile. I laugh a lot. I am very likable. I am tall, fit, stylish and beautiful. I have a handsome rich guy who loves me. You would think that I have a perfect life. Some women might even wish that they had my life. I am Elena, Alyona or Alex and I am a 'Happy Mess'.

CHAPTER 4

From New York to LA or "How I lost Everything"

"When I was 5 years old, my mother always told me that happiness was the key to life. When I went to school, they asked me what I wanted to be when I grew up. I wrote down 'happy'. They told me I didn't understand the assignment, and I told them they didn't understand life."
~ *John Lennon*

I find it hard to write this chapter. It isn't fun to look at my life just a few years ago and describe what went wrong and how bad things got. It feels like such a deep, dark dream, but thankfully it is no longer a part of my reality. It is much easier to share how truly happy I am now than to revisit old struggles. Nevertheless, I do feel called to talk about my darkest times in hopes that someone might get "inspired" by them and find the healing that I found. I truly believe that if God gives you challenges, it is only because you can overcome them, get stronger, and go on to inspire others. You have to believe that, and you have to tell your story. Even if you think that no one cares, or no one else has gone through what you went through, you are wrong. Tell your story! It may help one person, two people or one million! Quantity is not as important as quality. If one person's life changes because you shared your struggles and then your victory over those struggles, it is already more than enough.

Let me start out by saying that Binge Eating Disorder was recognized in 2013 as a real medical condition. It is the most common eating disorder among United States adults, and about 2.8 million people are struggling with it. I am sure there are millions and millions of people around the world who are stuffing themselves with some kind of food right now to ease their emotional and/or physical pain, and hating themselves for not being able to stop at one piece of cake, candy or an ice cream bar, like I did. I remember trying to explain to my family why in one sitting I would eat an entire gallon of ice cream that my mother had bought for everyone to share and that should have lasted a week. I would say, "I feel like a drug addict and I honestly can't stop. I wish I could, but I can't. I just need to eat something sweet and I need to eat it all. The only thing that I think about all day long is sugar and when I will have my next fix. I feel like sugar and carbs are my only real friends in this world..." My family would look at me with such perplexed faces and tell me to stop this behavior and to not make a big deal out of it. I was not a drug addict, they would say, and that it was all in my head.

They thought that I just needed to apply my will power in order to change my eating habits. I am sure that many of you who are going through the same struggle as me know that it is not possible to "just" stop that behavior and that it is not "all in your head." However, to someone who has never been affected by a sugar addiction, it might look like a weakness and that's okay, I get that.

According to the World Health Organization, there are more than 350 million people of all ages who suffer from depression in the world. There are over 5 million people in the United States alone with different types of Obsessive Compulsive Disorder and it affects 1 in every 100 children. According to the National Institute of Mental Health, Bipolar Disorder affects approximately 5.7 million adult Americans, or roughly 2.6% of the US population from the age of 18 and older every year. I am sure there are millions more in the world that suffer from low self-esteem, lack of confidence and who have no idea what self-love feels like. Unfortunately, there are many more millions of people out there who were sexually abused or molested in their lifetime, and who still suffer today even if the abuse ended years ago. Sexual abuse and molestation by strangers and people that I knew and trusted over the years growing up also added to my lifetime of depression and emotional challenges. I know how this feels to think that something is wrong with you, and that you will never be able to get out of this cycle of darkness. Yet I also know now that there is a way out, and that you do not have to suffer all your life because of the negative things that happened to you in the past. That is why I feel the need to share my story.

So here we go — the not so pretty truth about how things went down on my road of transformation from a 'Happy Mess' to happiness. This is where my story from New York to LA starts. My life as I knew it was over. I left Tom. Actually, Tom left me. I was unhappy for so long in the relationship, but I just couldn't pull the trigger and end it. One day we went to see the movie The Blind Side and I became convinced that I would be happier if I adopted an African American kid, like Sandra Bullock did in the movie. When I shared this with Tom, he said that he didn't want to adopt a baby. If adoption was something that I couldn't live without, we had to break up and needed to move out so he could move on. Can you believe it? He wanted me to move out from our beautiful sunlit apartment overlooking Park Avenue and Union Square. I was absolutely heartbroken. Sure, I was unhappy with Tom for a long time, but I still loved him in my own version of what love was to me, and I was hoping that he would not let me go so easily over an adoption issue. The truth is that he also had probably been unhappy for a very long time with me. The baby was just an excuse for both of us to end our relationship. After some tearful conversations that led no-where, I moved out. Not only was this separation very painful, I was blissfully unaware of what else was coming my way as I had full confidence that money and jobs would always come to me easily, as they had in the past.

To begin my new life as a single woman, I decided to spend a summer in the Hamptons, drinking a lot of champagne so that I would not think about Tom. During that time, I had already met my spiritual teacher Dr. Levry, the founder of Naam Yoga, in NYC. Dr. Levry, the Naam Yoga studio and many students from the New York Naam Yoga community were all moving to Santa Monica. After the summer was over, I decided to follow them to the new Naam Yoga Los Angeles center to study more with Dr. Levry. When I got to Santa Monica, I rented the most expensive ocean view, beachside apartment that I could find. It was called the "Sea Castle." I took it right away because I loved the word "Castle" and I loved paying a lot of money. It felt good and I was used to having everything be the very best. I lived with many famous people in the building and I felt fabu-lous. I tipped the valet guys at least one hundred dollars each on Christmas and other holidays because that was what Tom and I used to do. They probably thought that I was a famous star from Russia or a trust fund baby, or maybe had a rich boy-friend. As silly as it may sound, it never crossed my mind that I wouldn't be able to sustain my elaborate lifestyle. Even though Tom was no longer in the picture, I still thought that there was an endless supply of money. At that point I had not worked in a few years and I was not sure how to fit a job into my busy schedule of shopping, laying out on the beach and working out with my trainer. Yes, that was my life I was used to back then... Thankfully I did at least something productive that first year in LA. I dove very deeply into my Naam yoga studies and took all of the trainings that Naam Yoga LA offered and also meditated for two hours each day, trying to clean out all of my mental garbage and heal from my depression as fast as I could. Naam Yoga was changing me and healing me. At the same time, I developed and produced a DVD program called "Naam Yoga Therapies for Happiness" to help people heal from depression and emotional challenges. Without any income, I was burning through my savings like fire. I didn't realize that there was no bottomless Amex card to support my love of Barneys, Saks and all of the great chic Montana Avenue boutiques, and that the way I was living could not go on for long. I didn't think about the future, I just kept spending extravagantly. One day, about a year after I had moved to Los Angeles, the money was all gone. There was no notice, no goodbye — just gone. At that point, I was teaching at Naam Yoga Los Angeles twice a week and selling my DVDs online and in few stores, but that was all that I was doing to earn money and it wasn't much. I found myself officially broke and living in one of the most expensive apartment buildings in Santa Monica. My lifestyle of Whole Foods, Urth Cafe's takeouts and expensive organic lattes was "superstar" worthy, only it wasn't possible anymore. I was desperate. I had to find a job immediately. I called everyone I knew from my yoga center asking for connections in any industry. I was ready to take any job as long as someone could hire me right away, which was my only requirement. A yoga friend of mine told me that her boyfriend sold cars and that they were always hiring salespeople. I said fine, I'd see him tomorrow. So I did, and I got hired that very day — to sell cars! The only thing that I knew about cars was that they come in different colors and that they were a rather useful invention. I had never even owned my own car; I just rented one a few times when I moved to LA. Needless to say, I was definitely a fish out of water at the dealership and terrible at the job. By some sheer luck or maybe because someone took pity on me, I sold four cars during my first month. My eyes probably told the whole story, "If you don't buy this car, I am so fired." I didn't know a single thing about the cars I was selling, even after the training I received. I was fired within the first month. I had never been fired from a job before, so it was very upsetting. Little did I know that it was only the beginning of a long line of being let go from pretty much-every job I would have for the next 4 years, beside teaching Naam Yoga, which I considered my life and joy, not a job. I found out later from a friend at the dealership that the general manager there fired me because he thought that I was loaded and only took the job out of boredom. Where would he get that idea? I wore designer clothes to work, I lived in one of the best buildings in Santa Monica and I never inquired about my salary at the interview. When I took that job, it said that it paid $10 an hour and there is no way I could live like I did and make so little money, especially from an outsider's perspective. The truth was that I was just happy that someone hired me. I didn't care how much I was being paid as long as I was getting something. I had to sublet my apartment and live with a neighbor a floor below me, because my dealership salary wouldn't cover my rent any-way. Well, back to being unemployed and out of money again, I had so many bills piled up and I didn't know how in the world I got there and how I was going to get out. The only thing that I could do to keep myself sane was my Naam Yoga meditation practice each morning and evening. It helped me to have the faith and peace of mind to feel that somehow everything was going to work out for me one day.

CHAPTER 5

My Naam Beginnings

Before I go any further, I think I owe it to you to explain this "Naam" stuff in a little more detail. Naam Yoga was founded by Dr. Joseph Michael Levry, a great mystic, Kabbalah Master and creator of the Harmonyum Healing System. This advanced practice, the full name of which is "Shakti Naam Yoga", was instrumental in my healing process. It consists of working with Shakti force — the universal creative power, chanting the Divine Word (Naam), working with hand mudras, yoga movements, breathing techniques, and secret ancient yogic and mystical wisdom and meditations. It combines both Eastern and Western practices to help practitioners incorporate the true nature of the Divine in their lives. Naam is a Sanskrit word whose literal translation is "word" or "name." In Naam Yoga, we do specific Naam meditations using words from many different languages and backgrounds known to have a significant impact upon our consciousness. Therefore, Naam Yoga is as much a physical as it is a spiritual discipline. When practiced on a regular basis, it can help one to develop mental and physical strength, as well as enhance one's emotional wellbeing, intuition and creativity, and keeps you looking young and radiant. If you would like to know in more detail about the lineage of Shakti Naam Yoga, I suggest reading "Shakti Naam Yoga" by Dr. Levry, where you can also learn hundreds of techniques and meditations for health and blessings.

For those of you who might not know, the term 'mudra' refers to the manner in which our hands and fingers are positioned to induce a specific change in our health, our consciousness and even our level of prosperity. They have been prescribed by saints and sages for centuries for various illnesses, emotional problems and even as measures for softening many of life's challenges. "Our hands are the most powerful spiritual friends and helpers that we have. By working with the forces hidden in our hands, everything within us will become organized and harmonious. They will allow you to introduce balance and harmony into your life. Every time you need help you can do a particular mudra and develop the qualities of energy it contains. Thousands of mudras exist. Choosing the appropriate mudra and executing it properly can bring about miraculous improvements in the human body" (Dr. Levry, The Code of the Masters). I hope you will greatly benefit from the powerful technology of Naam Yoga and incorporate it into your life for your own healing and well-being. It will help you live your life to its fullest level of creativity, happiness and joy, as well as help you to serve and uplift others.

I happened to stumble upon Naam Yoga in 2010, thanks to my modeling agent and now dear friend Malissa Young who is a long-time student of Dr. Levry's. I came into her office to sign up with the agency and was completely mesmerized by the music that she was playing. It happened to be one of Dr. Levry's therapeutic "Naam" meditation CDs. Malissa highly recommended that I go see him personally so that he could give me my own private meditation practice. After meeting Dr. Levry and embracing the teachings that Naam Yogis refer to as Divine Spiritual Wisdom, I can now confidently say that Naam Yoga was and is the best thing that ever happened to me. It gave me an ability to transform, understand and accept myself like no other teaching or therapy ever could. As you know by now, I tried a lot of different things before I found it! Dr. Levry is an authentic Spiritual Master who studied with many enlightened Masters over many years. He is a wise, loving, unconditional and a fun teacher who sees and brings out the best in you, before you can even see it in yourself. Naam Yoga has so many spiritual tools to transform any condition, physical or emotional, that one might be battling with, that I know it is my duty to share what I know with all of my readers so that you too can have a platform for self-healing in your life. You too can transform any darkness in your life into light. Naam has filled my heart with unconditional love, peace and light, and continues to create miracles in my life, even years later. I went to my first Naam class as a lost, confused, angry and lonely girl in NYC, unable to deal well with life and with my negative thoughts and emotions. I did not even want to have people sitting close to me, yet alone to be nice to them. Yet everyone I met at the center was so unconditionally kind to me that eventually I couldn't help but to soften up. I had never meditated with mantras or practiced any type of breath work before in my life, so the first class looked completely foreign to me yet I could not deny the power of it. Every day, since that very first class, I have done Naam in some shape or form. Seven months after my first class I was floored by the realization that I was a completely different person. More accurately said, I felt like a real true me, able to put the expectations of family, society and even (most of the time) my own ego aside and truly enjoy being authentic and being myself. I started to feel carefree, happy and comfortable with expressing who I was, and people noticed. They would come up to me and ask me to share the "magic pill" I was on. They wanted to know why I was so happy. Why wasn't I worried about anything? All I could say to them was, "I do Naam".

At the end of the book you will find more information on Naam Yoga including every day techniques that are easy to apply to your life. I will also share with you where to find my Naam Yoga Therapies for Happiness DVD program whose techniques I used personally and later put on video specifically to help people deal with depression, to develop self-love and self esteem and to let go of past hurts and negative programming. It is a very short and simple program and in as little as twenty minutes a day it will do wonders for your well-being. Ideally this practice can be done for 120 days straight in order to get rid of old habits. This reasoning is based on the knowledge that it takes 40 days to erase old habits, 40 days to create new ones, and 40 more days to "seal the deal". Any real change requires a commitment of time. Don't worry though; even by doing it several times I am positive that you will notice a significant shift. You will be radiating light, happiness and such a powerful positive energy around you, that others will start noticing it as well. At first the practice might seem strange to you — chanting, mudras, and prayers in languages you might not understand — it probably looks weird to a lot of us Westerners. It certainly did to me when I first started. Truthfully, at times, I did not always feel the "heart opening energy rushing through my body" that some students would describe after class. Still, something in my heart kept telling me to continue showing up and sticking with it. One day, few months into my Naam Yoga practices, I felt a powerful shift during a teacher training. It all made sense to me after that moment. I started to feel more and more happy and connected to the Higher Power, more open to give and to receive love and joy. I became a true believer that Naam creates miracles and I simply cannot imagine not doing it every day now.

Speaking about "never say never," let's rewind to six months before I took my first Naam class. In my usual detox-spa-junky fashion, I was at the American Yogini retreat in the Hamptons, when the owner of the retreat showed me a book by Dr. Levry called "Lifting the Veil." It had many pictures and descriptions of meditations and mudras and she suggested that I try them. I flat out told her that she would never catch me doing something that "weird". In my head I thought I was "way too cool" for that. Now, here I am meditating every day, serving as a poster child for the saying: "never say never". Thank God the Universe was persistent and didn't give up on my healing process.

As it happens, the teachings and techniques in Naam Yoga are very sophisticated and there is so much one can learn from this practice that I cannot even try to do it justice in one tiny book. I just want to give you a little taste of it with few simple exercises and Naam meditations targeting the elimination of depression and other mental blocks. After that, it is up to you to see if this is something that you want to learn more about and make it a part of your daily practice.

*If you would like guidance on how to perform meditations from this book please visit: **www.elena.la** for a free video program.*

CHAPTER 6

The Power of the Universe: LA Style

One day at my car sales job, I had a profound experience that taught me about the power of the Universe and how it always has your back. I had no money whatsoever left in my bank account and I couldn't pick up my paycheck until the next day. I didn't have any food or any money. I didn't want to reach out to anyone I knew, as I did not feel comfortable disclosing how bad things really were. As I clocked out for lunch, I sent a prayer to God to help me figure out how and what I was going to eat. The moment I stepped out from the building, my cell phone rang. A guy I had dated for a few months when I first moved to LA called out of the blue with these exact words, "I am in Santa Monica sitting down to eat lunch and for some reason you came into my mind. Would you care to join me? My treat." You can only imagine how I felt, "Ask and you shall receive!" The Universal Law put into action. I had always believed in that law, but never had it working for me quite that fast before. That is how powerful the Universe is when you have faith and resist the temptation of worry. I worried plenty before in my life, but that day I remember being super calm about the situation, knowing that somehow it all had to work out. As a last resort, I could eat all of the cookies the dealership kept out for customers in the showroom. It was extremely humbling to realize what a financial mess I had gotten myself into and to feel what those truly in need of food must go through each day. It was a much-needed experience. It's not that I was a spoiled snob my whole life. After all, I grew up in the Soviet Union waiting in food lines and relying upon rationing coupons. My family and I were on food stamps when we first moved to Toronto and yet somehow I managed to forget it all. I got so used to the lifestyle of not looking at prices and buying whatever I wanted to at any time I wanted. They say you can get used to the good life very fast and I sure did.

When we develop a feeling of deep, unshakable trust and faith in the Universe, we automatically attract that which we desire or even something better, since we are not worried about when it is coming and how it is going to happen. It is through strong, 100% faith that we develop a power to manifest our unseen desires, without any previous physical evidence of those desires being manifested. In fact, we create that evidence through the act of our faith. Faith can see results before they happen, while belief still needs evidence. When you truly know in your heart that you are a beloved child of the abundant Universe, and that your loving parent, the Universe, God, Higher Power or whatever you have faith in, will not let you go without, you create a strong magnetic quality in your energy field which starts bringing you that which you asked for. Through the Grace of the Divine, I was able to tap into that Law that day and it manifested instantly when I needed lunch. It took me a long time until I fully realized that this was my only job — to have one hundred percent faith in what the Universe hears all of my needs, knows my heart, and will always provide and will never let me down, ever. When I finally realized this Universal Law, that you can manifest anything in life by having unshakable faith that you will have that which you desire, my entire life was changed forever. Of course I am still on the journey of mastering it. I have good days, filled with faith, and bad days, full of worry and fear. I just know that my job is to remember and hang on to this Universal Truth and it will not let me down.

Know that this Law will always be working for you, like the Law of Gravity. It is immutable. It cannot be silenced. What you have faith in, or something even better will always be given to you in divine time. The only reason you do not have what you want is that you do not have one hundred percent strong faith that you can have it. Your only responsibility is to trust the process and the timing of the manifestation of your desire, and at the same time to feel peaceful and calm while your desire is on its way into your physical reality. Do your best to have faith in the power of the Universe to always provide for you. See the final outcome and feel the way you want to feel once your wish is already fulfilled. You do not need to know about how it will be done, leave that part to the Universe to surprise you. You just need to be ready and willing to receive your desire, for Divine Intelligence goes where it is expected. I must say that often times what we do not get, is the result of the Universe's unlimited understanding that our want might actually hurt us. Therefore it is just as important to be thankful for what we "don't have" as what we do have.

CHAPTER 7

Sometimes Bad Luck is Good Luck

"Every problem is a solution to a bigger problem." – Dr. Joseph Michael Levry

In a way, I was relieved when I was fired from my car sales position. I truly hated that job. Sometimes bad luck is actually good luck. It just didn't feel good at the time. I was more broke after I lost the job, so I had to find another job fast. The next day, I took my resume to every store in the Santa Monica Place mall. That's right, the girl who once thought shopping in Bloomingdales was equal to being seen in Wal-Mart, the girl who considered Helmut Lang dresses her errand-running attire, was now hoping to get a job at the mall. The Universe has a great sense of humor. I was hired right away as the manager of a cosmetic counter. I had never put makeup on people before. I was the one that other people put makeup on. In fact, my makeup artist in New York was and still is the personal makeup artist to Melania and Ivanka Trump. Now I was the one putting makeup on people and doing mini facials — what a joke, I thought. Don't even ask me why they hired me without any experience in cosmetics or facial care. I guess I am just good at talking. I might have exaggerated a little bit about my make up application skills at the interview. Still the job didn't do much in the way of helping my financial situation. My entire salary was going into my astronomically high rent in my fancy "Castle" by the beach because renting it "undercover" on Airbnb was no longer an option, according to the management. As soon as my lease was over, I moved out of my overpriced apartment and moved into the guesthouse of a woman I had met in a bar just a few days before it. No joke. We met in a trendy bar in West Hollywood. I was out on the town with Peter visiting from New York. We went to Sur Lounge as Peter was in love with all of the good-looking bartenders who worked there. We were going to the LA Tony Awards Viewing the next day, where I was to be the date of the event's host, Tommy Tune, a ten times Tony Award winning Broadway legend. A girl at the bar overheard us talking about me trying to figure out what to wear for the red carpet the next day and offered her styling services in exchange for me saying to the press that she was my stylist. She styled me the next morning into a gorgeous red gown with a full open back and Chanel earrings. She ordered me a driver. When I came back to return the earrings (she let me keep my stunning one of a kind gown!) she found out that I had nowhere to live and offered to let me move in with her. She was a godsend to me at that moment in my life. Unfortunately, she turned out to be a drug addict and an alcoholic. It was hard for me to stay there and continue my yogic lifestyle of sunrise meditations and going to bed early. She constantly needed my company to hang out and drink with her and her friends, most of whom were addicted to drugs and alcohol as well. I lasted three months there, burning a lot of sage and incense but found myself hardly ever meditating and often drinking wine with her for breakfast. I really had to move out ASAP. That was a humbling experience, because I had to leave right away to save myself and still had nowhere to go. I could not ask anyone in LA for help because I already owed money to many of my friends. I was not making enough at the mall to pay for my own apartment or even rent a room. I didn't feel comfortable reaching out to my friends in NYC for help either. I didn't want to bother anyone with my problems. I began researching homeless shelters in LA and seriously considered going to one. As I was mentally preparing for that experience and moving my belongings into storage, my phone rang and one of my friends offered me to stay on his couch rent-free. At that time, I learned how people must feel when they are homeless and have nowhere to go and no one to turn to. It was another beautiful lesson, even though it surely did not feel like one back then.

You can see how much my life has changed in just a little over a year. I had no money, lived on a friend's couch and was still grieving over my breakup with Tom. I had not spoken to him in a year at that point. Trust me, there were many days when I wanted to reach out and ask him to get back together. I would tell him that we didn't have to adopt a baby anymore. I was lonely. I missed him and my luxurious life of abundance and privilege. I missed Saks Fifth Avenue. I missed Barneys New York. I missed my Platinum Amex card. Yet, even during those most challenging times, I still somehow managed to feel happier and calmer than I used to in NYC with all of the financial security and a good partner by my side. There were days when I was down, worried, lonely and sad, and even then, I was still okay. I was not fully devastated or depressed, just sad. Not miserable or hopeless and certainly not suicidal like I used to be before my life of Naam Yoga and spiritual healing. I kept up my practice of meditating daily with the special meditations from Dr. Levry and received Harmonyum Healing treatments once a week. Somehow, those practices carried me through the clouds of my life in a graceful way. I had no other choice but to pray "my butt off" every day and to be disciplined with my meditations if I wanted to, as Dr. Levry says, "stop the birds of karma from making a nest in my hair." My eating binges and face picking virtually disappeared from my life without any internal fight,

something I had never thought possible. I still had small epi-
sodes of both, but they happened much more seldom. I knew
that the new life I had in LA was better compared to my life in
NYC even though it came with lack, scarcity, and many new
challenges. My life in New York was full of material attachment,
luxury and yet complete confusion. I was just pretending. I was
not happy, not even when I was buying something new at Barneys. It was not working. Here in LA, I started to feel like I was
a little baby, learning for the very first time in my life how to
speak kindly about myself, what self-love must feel like, how to
be positive and how to have faith that everything that was happening to me was a part of the greater Universal plan, and that
everything was going to work out in the end, no matter how
bad it might seem at the moment. I was learning to trust in the
Universal Wisdom that sometimes bad luck is just plain good
luck.

This situation of living on a friend's couch was another
blessing. Everything I perceived as negative turned out to be for
my highest good. While living in his living room, we became
better friends and decided to open an apartment rental business
together. I borrowed some money from my girlfriend in NYC,
who became my mentor in that venture. My friend invested
some of his money. This is how the "HappyNess Hotel" was
born. We would rent out furnished apartments to tourists for

the next three years. We started with one, and grew to five apartments, a total of twelve rooms. I lived in one of the apartments, and we were constantly at full capacity. Sometimes I had to rent out my personal room and sleep on the floor in the living room. On many occasions during our beginning stages, I was sleeping on the floor. I was just grateful for having money in my pocket again after a long year of being broke.

People really enjoyed the way our apartments were decorated — full of bright green and yellow colors, with paintings, pillows, notes on the bedside tables that would remind them to smile, think positive thoughts and be grateful. We provided free access to Naam Yoga classes, another big reason why people visiting Santa Monica were trying to book their stay with us.

If you remember I was sharing how I did not like to clean. I had a housekeeper in NYC and in my pre-Tom life in Toronto. In LA, running the "HappyNess Hotel" by myself, I had to clean up to five rooms and bathrooms a day, and check people in at random hours. That situation was so ironic now that I was a cleaning lady on top of all the other hats I wore during the day. I remember being not so nice to our housekeeper in NYC if she would not hang my clothes properly after doing laundry. Now I know when I am blessed with such a luxury again, I am going to be grateful for all the help. I also never had roommates before living with Tom, because I hated sharing my personal space with people. Now I was living in the same apartment with three to five strangers at a time. I was just grateful that I had a roof over my head and did not have to sleep in a shelter or on a friend's couch. Those three years provided an incredible experience of humility and afforded me to have some money and meet hundreds of great people from all over the world.

One day in 2015, the short-term rental laws of Santa Monica had changed and we were forced to let go off all the apartments at a moment's notice. I was without money again. Instead of trying to get some kind of random job out of fear again, I decided that I just had to put all my trust in the Universe to guide me towards my true purpose in life. There were so many times I was shown while living in LA that every problem was a solution to a bigger problem. Bad luck would turn into a good luck eventually in some unexpected way. I had to start finally listening and paying attention to the signs and to not be afraid anymore to go for the life of my dreams. This meant not working for someone else, or being a "Maid in LA" (that was what Peter and John used to call me while I was running the "HappyNess Hotel"), and to really go for my higher destiny, which I knew was sharing Naam Yoga and Divine Spiritual Wisdom with others.

CHAPTER 8

Be Grateful For What You Have or You Will Lose It

When you are in the middle of turbulence and going through a rough patch in your life, it is often very difficult to be able to the see the blessing in the midst of your struggles. Only now, years after my life as I knew it started to crumble, I started to see why I had to lose everything — love, money, and even my fit body (I gained fifteen pounds in the first year and a half in LA). It all had to take place because I was never grateful for all of the blessings that I had in my life. I had to lose it all so that I could learn how to practice genuine gratitude! As I mentioned earlier, I did not even think about being grateful in the past. I always took the good things and people in my life for granted. Not until my third year into my Naam Yoga practice, when I went on a magnificent, soul awakening seven-day Divine Spiritual Alchemy retreat with Dr. Levry in Los Cabos, that something incredible happened to me. One day, all of a sudden, my heart started to overflow with appreciation for a server who brought me my latte in the morning, for a maid cleaning my room, and for Dr. Levry's lectures on Divine Spiritual Wisdom that he generously shared with us each evening. I was feeling that strange, heart-opening and overwhelming feeling of gratitude for everything and everyone for the very first time in my life and it felt really good. I never knew before what appreciating something or someone really felt like. I took all of the blessings in my life before as a norm, thinking that this was how life should be. I felt entitled to things and never for once thought that I was actually blessed to have health, good looks, money, love, family, friends, opportunities, etc. In fact, I was always looking at what was wrong with my life and the people in it. I loved complaining. Seeing what was wrong was easy, but being grateful and focusing on the positive and good things in my life was not even a thought before that trip. There is a spiritual Law that says that what we do not appreciate we will lose. That is exactly what happened to me. I lost almost everything that I had and I found myself in LA, single, broke, far away from my family and closest friends and on top of it all, I was chubbier!

It is very funny how life teaches you gratitude and appreciation. I could have never learned this principle if I did not lose it all. I wish that I was born and raised with those feelings already built in so that I would not have to learn the hard way to count my blessings. I wish there had been a course in my school, somewhere amidst chemistry, biology, math and geography called "How to be grateful so that you can lead a happy life." We spend so many years in school, in my opinion, learning things that in real life have little value. If you ask me, I would much rather be life smart than book smart. Meditation, Laws of the Universe, self love, yoga and other subjects on personal development are necessary things to understand when you are growing up. Yet it is better to learn later in life than never, like in my case.

I am so grateful for my "Gratitude Degree", even if it meant a lot of pain and suffering. As they say, you have to go through fire to become gold. Now I do my best every day to be consciously grateful for everything — for a discount at the dry cleaners, a coupon from a local dentist, the sun in the sky, LA's amazing weather, walks on the beach, the ability to buy food, my car, a roof over my head, my own bed, my health, the health of my loved ones, you name it — I am grateful for it. This is not something you become perfect at overnight. Like a muscle, it requires training and effort to keep cultivating an attitude of gratitude and appreciation for even the smallest blessings that we have. For me, it is a continuous conscious choice that I have to make — instead of complaining about my problems and worrying, I must decide every day to take a personal responsibility. Since I want a beautiful life, I need to focus on gratitude and on what I have versus what I don't have. Grateful. Grateful. Grateful. I AM.

I invite you, if you are going to take only one thing out of this book, to start focusing on being grateful. Even if you never do Naam, just by being grateful every day your health will improve, your relationships, your career and even your physical body will change for the best. You will become a much happier person. Trust me, there are many days when I have "to fake it before I make it" being grateful for my life but even faking it counts, because eventually being grateful will become your true nature. Go for it, and see the magical energy of gratitude start to eat darkness out of your life.

CHAPTER 9

How My Inner Chatter Became My Reality

I would like to take a moment here and share a little bit about that "mysterious" weight gain of mine. I clearly remember my Dad telling me one day when I was wearing a short skirt that I needed to tone my legs, and that I should not be wearing skirts until I did so. At the time, I was sixteen, in a great shape and did not need any toning up. My Dad was a perfectionist. I totally believed in his limited idea of me. From that day on his reality became my truth: I had fat legs and I was out of shape. I repeated this "truth" to myself over and over, either out loud or in my head. It did not help that at age nineteen I started modeling and was constantly told by the industry people that I needed to lose weight, that I was "big-boned", too muscular, and other similar things. I was so brainwashed by those opinions of other people about me that in my twenties I was constantly telling myself, "I am too fat. I need to lose weight. I am a big girl." I felt big, fat and ugly even though I was always a size four or six and because I was convinced my legs were too bulky, and not sexy, I didn't wear short skirts for many years. No matter how many bikini pictures I had in my modeling portfolio, no matter how much constant praise was given to me by my friends, I felt I was too big and unattractive. Even when my photos were in bridal magazines all over Canada representing one of the best Haute Couture designers in the country, I still thought I looked terrible and fat in them and the fact that they even wanted my pictures in magazines was some kind of an accident. Being sponsored by a successful modeling agency in New York City and granted a visa from the United States Government to immigrate to the USA from Canada under the special talent "model" category didn't change a thing in my mind. I continued to believe that I was fat and I could never understand how I got the visa in the first place. These thoughts became a prominent force in my everyday life. When someone would give me a compliment on Naam Yoga videos that I made I would always reply, "Oh no, I look so puffy and fat." I remember walking on the streets of New York, coming out of auditions and men would stop on the street to tell me how beautiful I was. All that I could think in my head was, "If only they knew how ugly and miserable I feel inside right now…" I became so convinced that I was fat and told myself that story for so long that finally I just started to gain weight. I didn't change my diet. I was still working out and yet I was getting bigger and bigger. No matter how much I dieted, juiced, completely starved myself and worked out, I could not lose those extra fifteen pounds I gained for many years.

What I did not know back then was another Universal Law that everything that you internally say to yourself, especially when mixed with strong emotion, will one day show up in your physical reality. Now that I know the power of our words, thoughts, feelings and inner chatter, and see how they shape my life and the lives of my friends, clients and students, I understand that I created that reality for myself by weakening my energy field with my own negative feelings and thoughts. Your words, spoken or internal, create your reality. Your thoughts create your feelings and everything that you think and feel about long enough, positive or negative, will eventually manifest itself on the physical plane. In other words, 'As above, so below'. There is no way around it. It took a lot of conscious work on my part in order to change how I talk to myself and how I feel about my body, for me to finally start losing weight and getting back to my healthy weight. When I gained that extra weight and would look at the old modeling pictures or yoga videos of myself, I would kick myself in the butt, wishing I could look how I used to look back then. What used to be "fat and ugly" to me just three years ago now looked like the "ideal me" and a dream goal to achieve.

I encourage you to take a moment throughout your day and slow down so you can hear your internal chatter. How you speak to yourself is the real you. If up until now you have been critical, negative or anything else but loving and positive toward yourself, it is time to turn that ship around. The truth is that fixing your inner chatter is completely within your power. Actually, you are the only one on Earth who can control it. No doctor can do it for you. No psychiatrist can do it for you. No pill can do it for you. The moment you become conscious and aware of your thoughts and feelings, you start to change and heal. It might take you some time and effort to transform your inner talk, but with patience and persistence it will happen and once you become sweet, loving, encouraging, kind and positive towards yourself, your outside reality will follow suit. Do not believe me, just try it for yourself and see what happens and how your life will transform. You will not be disappointed.

CHAPTER 10

The Law of Service

"Serve others and the Universe will serve you. Above all, remember that all you need to do is to touch one heart and you will create a ripple of love, peace, and light that extends beyond the radius of that initial interaction."
~ Dr. Joseph Michael Levry

So there you have it. I was once a girl who seemed to have it all. I lived a life of money, prestige and status in one of the world's most famous cities. In another famous city, I lived a life of poverty, humility and limitation. What did this experience teach me? Well, for starters, as the saying goes, I learned that "money can't buy happiness." It really can't. Over the years of being broke I still managed somehow to be the happiest, calmest and most peaceful person inside that I have ever been in my life, minus the millions of dollars in the bank account of my handsome and talented ex. I am not saying that I enjoyed a life of lack. Indeed, I think a life of lack is an unnatural state to human beings and is self-created by our limiting beliefs due to the environments in which we are raised, our internal chatter and the amount of self-love and self-worth that we feel. Yet I would not trade this life of material struggle for anything. I have many wealthy clients, just like I used to be, and they are very unhappy, just like I used to be. My goal today is a life of balance. I strive for balance in everything. I feel like a spiritual billionaire these days and I know that money alone will never make anyone happy. It all has to start with peace and joy from within. I truly believe that emotional stability and spiritual abundance triumph over financial stability and abundance. Thankfully, no one is asking us to choose. We all can have both spiritual abundance and financial abundance. I am grateful for the awareness that true happiness lies in the balance of both. You need to have financial stability, so you can have a luxury of time to study spirituality without being worried about paying for your basic needs. Yet, when you die, what counts the most is not how many cars, shoes, bags or diamond rings you may have had, but how many people you helped and how many hearts you have opened. To get there, the first stop is your own heart. You will know that your heart is open when you start seeing God in yourself, God in everyone you meet, even if they piss you off, and God in every spiritual teaching. When you have love and respect for yourself, others, and for every sacred text then you can say you are on the right path. At that point, your heart will be so full of love and compassion for the humankind that your main question in life will be: 'How can I serve?' Making my life matter through serving others has become the biggest source of joy for me in recent years. The only permanent thing in life is change, and change going through me feels like a hurricane at times. From Park Avenue to a close encounter with a Los Angeles homeless shelter — that is how far this change has brought me. Now I wake up every day being grateful for my life, a feeling I had no idea about just a few short years ago. I am the most positive and peaceful I have ever been, in my thoughts, words and attitudes. I have the opportunity to affect people's lives positively every day through teaching Naam Yoga classes and through my video programs. I get to work at the Naam Yoga International Headquarters in Santa Monica, a beautiful healing space four blocks from the ocean. It is a true privilege that I do not take for granted. I know that the life that I live these days is a very blessed one and it gives me an opportunity to help other people and to do what I love.

From a spiritual perspective, we know that the more challenges we have, the more service we should be doing. Many spiritual people, when facing challenges, dive into serving others. In India, people go to temples and serve by washing the floors and serving their spiritual community, in order to ease their challenges. Service is the fastest way to burn karma. It is said that when you serve others, the Universe shall serve you. It is another Spiritual Law — The Law of Service. If you are reading this book and feel that your life is in a funk and that you have even more challenges than anyone else in the world, ask yourself, 'How can I serve?' If you think you have nothing to give, like I used to think when I felt depressed and hopeless, this is the perfect opportunity to actually find a way to do just that — give. If you are unable to give financially, you can always give a smile, a hug or your time. Praying for someone else is a very powerful act of service and it is completely free! Sometimes the right words, a warm sincere smile, a compliment or a simple gesture of sincere interest in a person, is all a person needs to change the course of his or her life. My modeling manager, Malissa Young, played a huge role in the book of my life and all she did was make a simple suggestion that I see Dr. Levry and try a Naam Yoga class. It took her one minute to do that, but that minute changed my entire life. If it had not been for that crucial advice in my life, I might not even be here or I might still be the same negative self-destructive person. Never underestimate the power of your smile, a hug, a prayer or loving words of wisdom. You too can change someone's life at any moment. Ask yourself, "How I can serve?" Put service into action. You will love the results!

One of the most powerful prayers I learned in Naam Yoga Teachings is the prayer of Love, Peace and Light. Reciting this prayer every morning or before you go to bed will uplift you and add to the healing energy of the entire planet, as you are praying for every one in the Universe when you do it. Do not underestimate the power one person has to affect the entire world. Every word that you say, every thought you think and every feeling you feel adds to the collective energy of the world, and can be used for good, or for destruction and negativity. I work with this prayer every day after my morning and evening meditations, and in the end of every Naam Yoga class. I encourage you to learn it and use it to heal yourself and send Love, Peace and Light to everyone on our planet.

The Prayer of Love, Peace and Light

By Dr. Joseph Michael Levry

Love before me	Peace before me	Light before me
Love behind me	Peace behind me	Light behind me
Love at my left	Peace at my left	Light at my left
Love at my right	Peace at my right	Light at my right
Love above me	Peace above me	Light above me
Love below me	Peace below me	Light below me
Love in me	Peace in me	Light in me
Love in my surroundings	Peace in my surroundings	Light in my surroundings
Love to all	Peace to all	Light to all
Love to the Universe	Peace to the Universe	Light to the Universe

CHAPTER 11

Be Your Own Star

"It's all so mundane now. You know, what shoes they're wearing. 'Look, stars pick up dog poop!' Whatever those magazines are, they've so dumbed our country... And I think what people are doing is missing out on their lives by tuning into this fake celebrity s—t." ~ Chris Noth, Actor

Most people do not come to spirituality just so they can glorify God. They come because they have been down on their luck in life and they need true healing. Something caused them to suffer and that suffering brought them to their spiritual path, which cracked their hearts open. That is the exact pattern that led me to Naam Yoga and to healing of a lasting nature. I wish I was brought up as a kind, happy, grateful, spiritually conscious child with her heart full of love for the Creator, but I was not. As a young adult I lived a fast-paced materialistic life, full of excitement and glamour. At the same time, I was truly confused about life and felt angry and pessimistic. Life had to shake me up, force me to go through emotional challenges, family struggles, to lose money, love, career status and to gain weight just so I could wake up. No one can wake you up from the illusion of misery. You have to decide for yourself that you are no longer willing to live a life of adversity, negativity and poverty. Refuse to see yourself with any shortages. You have to break the pattern of thinking that life is hard or that someone else is having a better life than you. Instead, live your life as if it was easy, as if it was a playground, not a battlefield. We live in a modern world obsessed with the lives of other people, especially celebrities. If you want to be happy, you need to stop comparing your life to other people, and just enjoy the one that is yours. I used to do that a lot in the past, look at the lives of people from the outside and think that they were so much happier, healthier, and sexier. That pattern of thinking creates a low vibration in your cells and in your body because jealousy carries a low vibrational energy. In turn, it brings more negativity into your life and moves you even further away from all of the things that you desire. The first time I remember making a conscious effort to stop that pattern in myself was during a massage when I was staying at the Hippocrates Health Institute on one of my regular detoxing vacations. As a practitioner started to work on me, I began to complain about all of the things that I did not like about my body and how I wish I looked better. The masseuse stopped me in my tracks and shared a story of a patient who had been at the institute recently. She was in her twenties, and more beautiful than Angelina Jolie, according to the masseuse. She was married to a gorgeous, loving husband and they had two young twin boys. When you looked at her from the outside you would think that she was perfect and that her life was perfect. The reason she came to Hippocrates was because she was battling cancer. Not long after she completed her stay, she passed away. As my practitioner shared this story with me, I realized how ungrateful I was to complain about a few extra imaginary pounds on my belly when I was completely healthy. Most of us have done this at some point in our life. We look at the pictures of a stunning celebrity living the most glamorous life from the pages of the gossip magazine and we think how nice it would be to have her looks, money, boyfriend, etc. Perhaps you are reading that magazine in the store, because you can't even afford the five dollars to buy it, and you haven't had the money to buy a new dress or haven't gone on a date in over a year. I get it. I have been there. I am asking you now, like my masseuse asked me, to snap out of it. Stop criticizing your life and wishing you had someone else's. If you met me a few years ago, you would think that I had the best life ever. If you looked at my Facebook profile, you would be impressed with my travels and all of the fancy events I attended. As you know by now, I may have looked good on the outside, but I was dead on the inside. Do not wish to have someone else's life, just make sure you are living your own to your very best ability. Declare your intent for healing and have faith that what will be coming your way is going to be for your highest good, no matter how hard it might be at times to go through the journey.

For years I prayed for answers. I wrote letters to a higher power asking it to help me stop binging, damaging my face, drinking too much, being addicted to the pain and suffering and constantly finding myself in unhealthy romantic relationships. The solutions never came as fast as I hoped, yet I kept writing my letters, kept praying and waiting for a miracle of healing to finally happen to me someday. They say that the teacher comes when the student is ready, and Dr. Levry came into my life when I was no longer able to carry on in my old ways, when I knew that things had to change or I simply would not make it. Only then was I willing to do the work it required to change. If things were not as bad as they were, I would not have given all of my effort to my spiritual practice. I was blessed to receive a personal mantra meditation practice from Dr. Levry early in my spiritual journey. I did it religiously, morning and night, almost three hours a day total. I went to Naam Yoga classes almost every day for a year. I read Dr. Levry's books on Divine Spiritual Wisdom and dove into his trainings. I received the Harmonyum Healing energy treatment about once a week. (This energy healing is the most powerful system I have ever encountered and I tried many techniques in my search for healing over the years. It gently washes away all of your deep-rooted traumas and helps you to change in a permanent and conscious way. Harmonyum, combined with Naam Yoga allowed me to unmask and change my negative thought patterns. Once I brought consciousness to my thoughts, I was able to slowly but surely shift my negative patterns into positive ones. It is my favorite thing to do these days, to receive a Harmonyum, and I do not go more than a week without one. I will provide more information and a link to learn more about Harmonyum Healing later in the book.) Only seven months after I started receiving Harmonyum treatments, I felt my depression lift and my body heal. I had spinal injuries and 5 herniated discs from two car accidents and had been in chronic pain for eight years. The doctors said that there was nothing that could be done to heal my spine and yet Harmonyum Healing allowed my body to heal itself. I have been pain-free for years now and I am so grateful for it. I invite you to start believing that your body is a powerful self-healing instrument, and that no one can tell you what you and your body can or cannot do. Healing physical and mental illness starts in your mind, in how you are going to think and feel about your situation.

As you can see, it took me fifteen years of searching for answers, praying for help, and dreaming of a day when I would wake up and feel sincerely happy, beautiful, awesome and so in love with my life that I could finally stop being jealous of the seemingly fabulous lives of people in reality TV shows, monitoring the news on celebrities for updates in marriages, careers and success, living my life vicariously through their lives. I want to assure you that true happiness is within your reach too. I hope that my journey will assist you on your path, so that it will not take you fifteen years to understand that we are all born to be happy and that we all have the right "wiring" for happiness. Happiness is a gift from the Universe for you to partake in, no matter who you are or where you are in your life today. If you are not feeling all that happy today, know that you can and will get there, if happiness is what you truly want. You were born to shine, to create the life of your dreams and live it, enjoying every moment of this awesome creation. We all can be our own stars, in the reality of our own lives! You just have to make up your mind, do your work and never give up. That day will come.

CHAPTER 12

To Live and Love in LA (and Anywhere Else)

Since I moved from New York to LA five years ago, I find myself to be constantly single. When I lived in Toronto I used to get asked out on dates a lot and had a long-term relationship. Then there was my NYC life with Tom. So prior to moving to LA, I was constantly dating or in a relationship and I was looking forward to meeting new people and finding the right romantic partner in the 'City of Angels'. However, as soon as I got to LA, burning with desire to start a new life and get over Tom, it was as if the potential for any kind of romance came to a grinding halt. I really tried too. I went out to bars. I dated online. I shopped in Whole Foods every day — which seems like a popular place for singles to meet these days. My efforts resulted in only a few occasional dates, two of which were with guys from Whole Foods. I noticed a trend that the general comment from potential partners was that I was too spiritual for them, and that they could not handle my yogic lifestyle. The longer I searched, hoping and praying that the Universe would bring me my soulmate, the more I was setting myself up for disappointment.

From my years of study with Dr. Levry, and reading many books of other enlightened Spiritual Masters, I started to understand that the road I have taken is not a conventional one and definitely not the easiest, but it does lead to ultimate freedom and sustainable happiness. When you decide to devote your life to the search for the ultimate Truth, your light increases and you may no longer be a desirable partner to everyone you meet. You might be too much for them, too "out there", and not so fun to be with, if you don't like to party all night because you would rather wake up early the next day to meditate. Divine Spiritual Wisdom teaches us that we only see one percent of reality, the other ninety-nine percent of it is unseen. Many of us are placing all of our energies on caring for our physical bodies, our hair, our clothes, our cars, our homes, etc., in an effort to look good and be desirable to our current or future partner.

We are so preoccupied with the success of the physical reality, which we perceive as the only real reality. It is in truth only a shadow of the real, unseen reality. Many of us have souls that have not showered in years, if ever, and our spirits wear dirty clothes with holes in them and have very messy hair. I am saying this, not in an attempt to downplay what is happening in the physical world, but to awaken in you the understanding that, while it is important for you to care about your physical body, you are so much more than just your body. You are not your clothes, your makeup, or your car. You are an infinite spirit and you need your unseen bodies to be healthy and strong. Meditation, yoga, spiritual work, spending time with nature and animals, kindness and service to others are like manis and pedis or gym visits for your soul. The best shower for your invisible body is the discipline of thinking right, feeling right, speaking right, acting right and having a positive mental attitude toward life. All those aspects of your being are the unseen ninety-nine percent. They form physical life as you see it every day.

Your thoughts, words, speech, feelings, actions and attitude are seeds, the unseen causes of everything that you experience in your visible world, which is only the effect, or the fruit of those invisible forces. Most of us focus solely on the effect, trying so hard to change it, forgetting about what caused it in the first place and not realizing that in order to change the fruit you must change the seed. This is important for us all to understand. I was walking around for all these years in Los Angeles, working so hard every day on my spiritual development, spending hours in meditation and yet I was still looking for love through the one percent of me that is visible. I thought I had to be in a trendy bar on Friday nights, looking glamorous and stylish. If that particular bar did not work for me one week, I would try some other fancy place next week, hoping that my soul mate would show up there. I was convinced that I had to look sexy buying my wheatgrass juice so that some tall and handsome guy would notice me and ask me out and then we would live happily ever after. Of course I never met anyone I was interested in, but I kept trying. Let me break this down for you in spiritual terminology. I was eating the same fruit each week and each month, not liking the fruit and waiting for a different fruit to show up, not realizing that the issue was the seed, the cause — how I thought, felt and spoke about myself along with my actions and my attitude. Prior to my spiritual journey, I was mainly focusing on taking care of my physical body. It worked out for me for some time, but on a very superficial level. I attracted Tom, who thought I was beautiful and fit the profile of a perfect partner on every physical aspect. Even though I was freed from that shallow 'one percent' relationship of conditional love and limitations, I was looking for that same exact pattern, just in a different city, with someone new, hoping that it would somehow be better and end differently. I am sure that you have heard the saying, 'Insanity is doing the same thing over and over and expecting different results.'

What I had to realize after years of unsuccessful dating and sometimes very lonely nights with Netflix and ice cream is that I am more than one percent. I am more than just a perfect girl-friend to some perfect guy with a six-pack and a nice car. I am not just interested in fancy trips and spending our days drinking wine on a private beach any more. I am so much more than that now. I am no longer interested in superficial love, love that looks perfect from the outside, but is full of conditions and eventually disappointments and heartbreak. I do not want to repeat my experience with Tom with a new partner. Coming to this realization made so much sense as to why I am still single. If I am asking the Universe for my divine partner, who will love me unconditionally, who will see beyond the one percent of my physical body and admire and have reverence for my spirit, who will be an equal to me in his search for the Truth and spiritual freedom and service to humankind, then I needed to set myself free first. I decided to become free from negative thoughts and feelings about myself, free from self-sabotaging behavior, speech patterns and negative attitude toward my lack of ability to find "the one", free from the conditioning and limiting be-liefs that I developed early on in life about deserving to be loved, free from the collective belief that it is impossible to meet anyone in LA, and even free from the actual desire of fi-nally finding "the one". The longer I hang around with "want and need", the more "want and need" I keep creating in my life, successfully turning myself into a "lack magnet".

Spirituality teaches us that in order to receive anything we want in life, we need to learn how to give first. So if true love was what I was looking for, I had a task ahead of me to learn how to give to myself and to everyone I meet: family, friends, students, and even strangers.

This was the beginning of a new level of spiritual growth. I started asking myself questions, when buying groceries, "If I buy and eat this food, will it be an act of self love, or am I acting on my old patterns of self-destruction and sabotage?" I would ask the same type of question when invited out to a party, or anything else I would do — is this action a reflection of my self-love, or is this something that I do on autopilot, or out of some deep rooted insecurity, conditioning or pain? If the answer was yes and I was doing/eating/buying that thing out of uncondi-tional self-love, then I would do it. The results were magical — I was making healthier food choices and drinking less alcohol. I was only saying yes to things I really wanted to do and people I really wanted to spend time with. I was learning how to listen to myself and I was becoming aware of my thought patterns. It did not happen overnight. I am still a student on the road of mas-tering unconditional self-love. Even my initial questioning has resulted in many wonderful things. I started to cook for myself more. I took time to walk on the beach. I talked on the phone less. I started to learn to enjoy quality time with myself, instead of trying to be everything for everyone. I started to receive as much Harmonyum sessions as I could. That was helping me to become more aware of my thoughts, beliefs, feelings and choices. It felt amazing knowing that I was doing something nice for myself consciously out of love and care. I was not born in a country that cultivates self-love. My female role models, my dear mother and grandmothers, had really hard lives of living through a war, a communist regime, profound lack and turbulent times, where survival and the basic needs of their families was the only thing on their minds. Here I am in Los Angeles discovering what unconditional self-love feels like for the first time. When you start loving yourself and giving yourself the time and care you deserve, it heals all the generations behind us and the future generations to come. As I am writing this, my goal is to be a little bit better at being kinder, less judgmental and more unconditional toward myself every day. I hope to inspire you to do the same.

As for my not-happening dating life, I understand now that I can't expect to walk into a bar and meet a guy who will love me in the way I want to be loved — deeply, unconditionally, the type of love that only happens when the heavens bless you. In order to get there, I needed to learn how to give that love to others first, I needed to become an extension of Divine Love. For me, learning how to give love first meant walking down the street and smiling to strangers, silently blessing workers at the cash register or at the construction site I was passing by, blessing my friends and family before I went to sleep and so on and so forth. It meant that when someone was not so nice to me, I knew I had to make an effort to not react, and pretend that the only thing coming out of their mouth was, "Love, Love, Love". It meant seeing every object, every rock, every plant, every tree, every bird as a manifestation of the Divine and feeling love toward them and gratitude for their existence. It meant walking down the street and feeling grateful for the opportunity to feel grateful, as I did not know this feeling in such depth ever before. It meant realizing how lucky I was just to be alive, to be able to walk and to see the sun above my head and feel its warmth. All of these things and more became ways for me to give my love to everyone.

If you are looking for love, spending your time and money signing up for the numerous online dating sites and apps, running from one date to another in hopes of meeting your soulmate, ask yourself first whether or not you have done your homework. Do you already approach yourself from a standpoint of self-love and full acceptance, or are you hoping for that "one and only" person to come along and prove you that you are lovable? Are you walking around filled with love in your heart for everyone and everything, ready to give and share that energy with others, or are you expecting for someone to show up and make your life all better by loving you? Give and you shall receive never fails, but the only way you will activate that Universal Law is when you give completely and unconditionally, not expecting anything in return. Last but not least, are you aware of your thoughts, feelings, words, actions and attitude? Do you think kind thoughts and feel good about yourself? Do you truly believe that you are beautiful inside and out, and that someone would be blessed to have you as a partner or do you feel unlovable and not good enough? Do you speak about yourself with love and positivity or are you cursing yourself and your life with every word that comes out of your mouth? If being negative is your comfort zone, it is now time to make a conscious effort to change that habit. Your words, thoughts, feelings, actions and attitude are the root of what is happening to you on the outside, in your visible life, and chances are that if you are still single and looking for love, or already are in a relationship that is not 100% what you want, there is still some cleaning you need to do at some level.

You can never be too positive. Just promise yourself that you will do your best to change and become a little bit better every day, so your every thought, feeling, word, action and attitude will gradually become uplifting and loving toward yourself and others.

You have to become your own biggest fan, be truly and sincerely in love with yourself. You must cultivate unconditional self-love in order to attract your divine partner. When you love yourself, you give others permission to love you and create a platform for self-healing. You want that. You want a real connection. Do not settle and do not lose faith, but do lose the attachment to finding your partner. Cultivate your own connection with the Divine and allow your heart to be opened and filled with unconditional love. When you love yourself and love your own company and are no longer desperate for someone to come in and make your life better, it will all fall into place. You will meet your partner effortlessly. It will be beautiful. There is nothing more powerful in the Universe than the energy of Love, and the whole Universe is kept together by Love. I invite you to join me on the journey of cultivating love inside of yourself first, in order to eventually see it being reflected in your physical reality.

CHAPTER 13

LA Happiness Times

Here I am, living a new life, a life of happiness in the City of Angels. In just a few short years, through the grace of the Divine, I was able to completely transform myself mentally and emotionally, heal my binge-eating disorder, OCD, severe depression and negative thinking by practicing Naam Yoga at least twice a week, doing my daily Naam meditation practice and receiving regular Harmonyum healing sessions. My relationship with my family is more loving and we have been able to heal and move on from years of hurt and pain. The Naam Yoga Therapies for Happiness DVD I created is now selling worldwide with translations in Russian and Spanish available. I recently created the "I Am Happy" Naam Yoga socks collection. Happy feet make people smile and that is the best reward for me. I travel internationally teaching Naam Yoga. I live in one of the most beautiful cities in the world, I work daily with the amazing Naam Yoga LA team and enjoy being part of a healing center that changes people's lives on a daily basis. I also have been privileged to attend Naam Yoga's extraordinary Super-classes led by Dr. Levry to spread peace. The most recent Su-perclass, in 2015, united 100,000 people (live and online) from all over the world in Mexico City. I cannot begin to tell you what a magnificent and transformative experience it was to be there in the magical vibration of that many people united to-gether in the heavenly vibrations of Naam meditation. During the weeks and months after this powerful event, I felt elevated and experienced a huge shift in my own cellular vibration. So this is my life these days, and I would not trade it for anything!

As you can see from this book, I had to work really hard to get to this place. I had to lose a lot of physical comforts in order to open my heart up to the Divine love and healing. Long gone are the days of Park Avenue living and Saks Fifth Avenue shopping. I am grateful that I did not have to live in a shelter, but on a friend's couch. I am grateful to shop in a second hand store and I get excited about "splurging" on a seven dollar purse. My $500 haircuts with the best stylist in New York are long gone. I am happy and grateful now when my friend who is a hairstylist trades a healing session for a haircut. The many prayers that I said at the checkout, praying that my card would go through, replaced my carefree relationship with my platinum Amex card. In just a few short years I have been on both ends of life and I now see what a blessing it all has been. I am much nicer, kinder and more compassionate. I do not freak out impatiently anymore when a person in front of me is paying for his food in pennies, as I sometimes had to do that. I am in peace with who I am, no matter if I am wearing a second-hand inexpensive dress or a high-end haute couture creation. Our clothes, bags, cars and homes do not define us. I pray that everyone reading this book is already in this place, or will soon find the path to get there, where they are not solely attached to the material part of life, because it is impermanent. When we die everything stays here. When your only desire, your only question is, "How can I serve and what can I do with my life to make the world better?" then you will find that everything you need will start coming to you. When you want nothing, you will be given everything. You will be centered, balanced and most of all… happy.

I am in a place in my spiritual path where it is all starting to make sense. When I was living through those times of spiritual growth with physical and financial struggles, I did not see how anything good could come out of such a mess. Today I know what a blessing it all was, as it softened me up, taught me how to reach out for help and how to be humble and grateful for the smallest blessings. I had to learn self-forgiveness for all of the mistakes I made that got me in such a bad shape financially. I promise you that whatever darkness you might be faced with in your life right now, it is temporary. You will have to do some work and dig deep within yourself, and it might not be easy at times, but know that there is no birth of consciousness without pain, the same as in childbirth. No matter if your challenge is big or small, it will pass and one day you too will be able to share your story of triumph with the world. Your weaknesses will become your greatest strengths. So chin up and smile right this moment. For real, smile! Smile at your life, smile because you have the breath of life in you, smile because everything is going to be better than you can even imagine. Make finding the Truth and Freedom your main goal in life, and do not give in to your conditioning and the pressures of society. Serve God, the Divine, whatever you call this Creative Force, and the Divine will serve you. Work on building light in your aura and finding the love for the Divine in your heart and you will never lack anything, ever. Even if it is at the last minute the Universe will rush in to save you. Everything you are looking for in life is attracted to your light. The light that you have in your electromagnetic field works like an invisible spiritual bank account. I was able to experience first hand how truly powerful that currency is. These days I would rather have both money and light, but if I had to choose, light always wins, as it can get you much further than money, as money is the currency in our physical reality but light is the currency in heaven. As we approach the practical part of this book where I will share with you my favorite Naam Yoga and other spiritual techniques, going deeper into the program that helped me to find my balance and happiness, I want to thank you again for reading my story. It is a privilege and an honor to live it, to find healing and now being able to share it with you. I am so forever grateful for all that I went through and would not change anything on my path. I invite and encourage you to practice the following program laid out in Part 2, "Elena's Practical Guidelines and Philosophy for Happiness", as it will transform your life just like it transformed mine. Don't believe me, just find out for yourself!

Peter, John and I in Miami 2010 where John came up with a "Happy Mess" term to describe my life.

Modeling in NYC Central Park in 2010, feeling ugly and miserable on the inside.

Modeling in NYC Central Park 2016, feeling happy and peaceful.

Teaching Shakti Naam Dance for Happiness class at the Divine Spiritual Alchemy
Retreat 2016

Me in the front of the International Headquaters for Naam Yoga in
Santa Monica,CA, 2016

Being HAPPY these days (no longer a MESS) and combining my two passions, yoga and modeling.

PART 2

Elena's Practical Guidelines and Philosophy for Happiness

You do not have to be an optimist. I certainly wasn't. Take it step by step and one day you will be the most positive person you know. I mean it. Here is how I did it. The stuff below is magic. It looks simple, but it works. Simplicity is Divinity. So let's get to it!

1. As soon as you wake up, before you even open your eyes, think positive thoughts.

I decided some time ago to start each day with a positive thought. Your first thought of the day is a seed from which fruit will grow. The question is do you want a sweet fruit or a bitter fruit? Obviously we all want the sweet one. That is why I do my very best to make each morning a positive one, as I want to sow seeds that will turn into the most delectable fruit. In other words, I want to have a beautiful day ahead of me and I know I can create it by thinking right!

When I first tried to start using this concept, I would wake up and think, "Oh boy, I am so tired!", or "I am so pissed off at so and so," or "I am worried about such and such", and then I would immediately say to myself, "Cancel. Delete. Reboot. Change that thought Elena, think about something positive right now!" I would then direct my thoughts to: "Thank you dear beloved God for this beautiful day, for that fact that I woke up. Thank you that I have the chance to experience this day and all of the opportunities within it. I am so grateful!" Over time this has become my second nature. I wake up being positive and grateful to God for giving me another day, another chance to create the life of my dreams, knowing that it is a privilege to be alive. So go ahead and make your first thought of the day a happy and optimistic one. By doing so you will maximize the opportunities that come your way and open the door to the full manifestation of your dreams.

Elena's Favorite Morning Ritual to make a pact with the Universe:

After I wake up and send my first thoughts into the Universe about my love and gratitude for God and for all of His creation, for my life, my family and their health, I go into the bathroom and I make a fist with my right hand. Looking at myself in the mirror and smiling, I shake my fist up and down as I say out loud (with convictions!) three times: "Today is a great day!" Sometimes I even jump up and down as I say it and get myself really excited. It is important to look into your eyes while saying it, as doing so makes an imprint in the subconscious mind.

2. Monitor your inner chatter monkey and don't let it be mean to you.

Most of us can pretend well enough to be positive, optimistic and happy at least for some time when we are facing internal or external challenges. We can all smile big and pretty on the outside and be crying on the inside. I did it for most of my life. As I mentioned in this book already, how you think about yourself and what your inner chatter is telling you, that little voice inside your head that is always talking to you, is the real you. Are you kind, sweet and positive with yourself? Or are you thinking, "You stupid loser! You will never amount to anything!" or "Look how fat you've become, no one will ever love you," or "You are so broke..." or whatever else you like to torment yourself with?

Your inner chatter and the deeply rooted beliefs that you have about yourself and the world outside of you will define your life, as your every thought, feeling and speech, repeated long enough, whether you want it or not, will sooner or later manifest in the physical body and in your life. Take a moment to think, "Would you talk to your loved ones the way you talk to yourself? Would you talk to your cute little puppy like that?" If your answer is 'no', then keep reading! I also was not always nice to myself. It took me years of conscious self-mastery to finally make friends with my inner self and teach her how to be nice. If I were to treat my friends the way I used to talk to myself in my head for all of those years, I would have lost all of my friends a long time ago. I used to be cruel, mean and simply awful inside, constantly judging, name-calling and criticizing myself. When I understood that my inner chatter was creating my reality, it became clear why my life was full of suffering, negativity and drama. What is even more interesting is that those thoughts and chatter were not even mine to begin with. I accepted them, but they were not mine. Different people in my life put them into my head over the years and I took them as my truth and they crippled me for way too long. If you do not see yourself as a loving, sweet, kind, beautiful, abundant and great person, you too are lying to yourself and you too are listening to the negative voices in your head that most likely are not even yours. You might not agree with me right now that you truly are loving, sweet and wonderful, as I myself thought this to be "crazy talk" before. After some work and practice you will see how much goodness there is in you. There is light and beauty in everyone. Goodness is our true human nature and it is our duty to discover that goodness in ourselves. Start seeing God in yourself first, and then you will see God in others too. When you see God in others, when you see them as goodness and love manifested, you take away their ability to hurt you. You also give them permission to be their best and to blossom. This is very important to know and understand, as it is the biggest gift you can give anyone. First, you have to start with yourself. Give yourself your unconditional support and acceptance. Know that you are doing your best and there is always tomorrow to try to be an even better person than today. There are great rewards for small steps.

One of my favorite quotes is by Oscar Wilde, "Every saint has a past and every sinner has a future." Forgive yourself for anything that you are not proud of, as going through that experience showed you where you needed to change. Know that once you bring light to any dusty corners of your life, you are bringing awareness to what needs to be cleaned. Do not be hard on yourself. Just keep trying to be a little bit better every day. It is so much more fun to like yourself than to hate, to praise than to criticize, and while still not perfect at it, I am enjoying every minute of being nice to myself these days. I invite you to join me!

Throughout my years of working with Naam Yoga and Divine Spiritual Wisdom, I had to become my own "Inner Chatter Police". When I first started this practice I was so over being a Happy Mess, living in pain, suffering, drama and misery that I began to actually enjoy the discipline of paying attention to my thoughts and to what I was saying to myself throughout the day. I now see the results of that monitoring in my daily life, with blessings coming and positive things happening to me all of the time. The more you do it, the easier it becomes to be conscious of your inner chatter and views about yourself and your life. Becoming conscious about something that might not be working for you anymore is the beginning of a profound change. I invite you to start monitoring your inner talk throughout the day. Are you looking at the bright side of a situation, which can always be found, or is your attitude more of a "glass half empty" one? Is your reality being manifested on autopilot, or are you being a conscious co-creator of it? Even if you are that "glass half empty" person, like I once was, when you start training yourself to speak to yourself with kindness, and to see blessings in everything that happens to you and realize that each problem is just a solution to a bigger problem, you are almost certain to wake up from limitations of this illusory reality and start living in a much brighter world, full of possibilities, positive and kind people, jobs and financial opportunities, perfect health, loving relationships and true happiness.

Elena's Three-Minute Positivity Booster

Right after I do my "Today is the best day!" affirmation, I make sure, while still looking at myself at the mirror, to spend anywhere from 30 seconds to 3 minutes, depending on my schedule that day, smiling at myself while saying something nice to myself. "I am beautiful, I am happy, I am healthy, I am rich, I am lovable, I am enough, I love myself and I love my body" are among my favorite morning affirmations. You can focus on just one and repeat it over and over (I have done that during specific times of my life, where I felt like I needed more concentration on the wealth or health areas, for example.) You can also create a number of your own affirmations. Smiling at yourself and telling yourself how much you love yourself and how amazing you are first thing in the morning will set a tone for your entire day to be filled with self love and positive feelings towards yourself. You really deserve it! Give this affirmation practice a try!

3. Clean your dishes every night.

Your happiness starts with you cleaning your own mental garbage. I am all for doctors, as they help a lot of people and going to the doctor can sometimes be exactly what you need. Still, no one, not even the best doctor in the world, can clean your negative mental programming, past memories and pessimistic inner chatter except you. Think of your negative past memories as dirty dishes. Every day you are given beautiful new fresh food to eat, but since you were too lazy the night before and did not clean your dishes, you cannot truly enjoy this delicious food that is sitting on your dirty leftover plate. We do this every day when we live our present life based upon our past perspective. You do not need to hang on to your past memories, unless they are super positive and uplifting. If your past is bringing you down, makes you not want to trust that your current boyfriend loves you because your ex cheated on you, or you think that you will be laid off from the job of your dreams, because you got fired from a job before, and that your colleagues do not like you, because when you were in school all the kids used to make fun of you, and so on - this is a true indication that you need to clean your dishes at night and wake up with a shiny clean new plate for your new day's blessings and experiences. It is time to let go, I am pretty sure you agree. But how, you might ask? Below is a personal story followed by a technique that worked for me to clean my "dirty dishes".

I remember during my darkest days I would feel so horrible about myself, filled with guilt, shame, self-hatred and terrible memories that I would search for hours on the Internet for a way to kill the part of the brain that controls painful memories. I looked for pills, surgery, anything. I know that it probably sounds crazy, but I was serious, as I could not cope with all the thoughts running through my head, such as, "You are a horrible, terrible, really, really bad person, Elena," and all the memories of my actions over the years and of all the people I hurt in the process in order to validate the deep, strong and very negative beliefs about myself. Sometimes those thoughts and feelings would keep me up all night, while I cried and wallowed in what a bad, hopeless, useless person I was. The saying, "For as he thinketh in his heart, so is he" (Proverbs 23:7), is as true as the Sun rising in the east. What I was thinking about myself was destroying me and destroying important relationships in my life. So, I searched and searched for a way to surgically fix my brain, but I could not find any medical solution to rid myself of those memories and thoughts. That is because, short of getting a lobotomy, the only person or thing that can wash the mind clean of the past is you.

While I was surfing the Internet trying to figure out how to free myself from my negative memories, I must have set some energy into motion. As we all probably have heard by now, our intentions are very powerful and my intention was to find a way out of the darkness and pain, because I had hit rock bottom. Even though my life at that time had been so privileged and blessed with material abundance and with a handsome, loving partner, emotionally I felt the lowest I have ever been. I really needed help, and thankfully no one was offering to perform the brain surgery that I was looking for. What was I thinking, wanting to have a brain surgery anyway? From where I am standing now, I almost can't believe that I was that serious about finding a way to do that just a few years ago.

As I was Googling night after night trying to find a surgeon, the Universe must have seen me going cuckoo and decided to have mercy on me. It was at that time that I found my spiritual teacher, Dr. Levry, and Naam yoga, a practice that saved my life, as you know by now. It was in one of those classes that I heard, for the first time, that your breath is the king of the mind, and your mind always follows the breath, and when you know how to breathe properly and control your mind, you can heal pretty much anything in the body, as any illness starts and ends in your mind.

I was searching so hard for some miracle cure for my mental suffering and was ready to pay any amount of money for it, while all of this time it was literally right under my nose and for free! I dove into the Naam teachings, went to classes almost every day and learned many different breathing techniques that helped me to calm my nerves, release negativity and change my emotional state. When I learned the powerful yogic breath that I am going to share with you below, I practiced it for the entire year almost every day with great results. I still use this breath occasionally in my personal practice and nearly always in my classes and sessions with clients.

Elena's Favorite Non-surgical Technique for Cleansing the Subconscious Mind of Traumatic Memories

Position: Sit in Easy Pose with your legs crossed (or you can sit on a chair with a straight spine). Have your arms bent by your sides with your index fingers pointing up and the rest of the hand making a fist (In this mudra, we are working with the index finger, whose energy corresponds to the planet Jupiter which brings happiness and prosperity). The eyes remain slightly open and relaxed, gazing softly at a point in front of you.

Breath: Inhale four segmented breaths through the nose and exhale one powerful and deep breath out of an "O" shaped mouth. It is a fast-paced breath. Practice for one to three minutes daily. With every exhale, imagine that you are releasing any unwanted memories from your life.

To End: Inhale deeply through the nose. Close the eyes. Suspend the breath for 5-15 seconds (unless you are pregnant or have high blood pressure), squeeze the pelvic floor muscles, and press your tongue against the upper palette. While you are holding the breath in this way, imagine beautiful white light all around you. Visualize yourself as happy and prosperous and doing what you love the most. Exhale through the nose. Then lift your hands up over the head, shake them vigorously, look up and laugh out loud, as loud as possible, and do not worry if you have to fake it, your brain does not know the difference. You will feel happier immediately.

4. Invoke the power of positive feelings to manifest your dreams.

Before going any further I have a question for you. Do you know what your perfect life would look like? Do you know exactly what you would be doing, where you would live, who you would be with, what car you would drive, what you would look like, your state of health, your attitude, your bank account, what you would do with your free time and so on and so forth? Believe it or not, when most people are asked this question, they have no idea, because they don't think this perfect life is possible, or they don't think that they deserve it. The reason I am asking you to consider your perfect life is because the Universe responds to order and clarity. In fact, the Universe is like a computer and you are the programmer. You need to know what kind of program you want and create clarity around it in your mind in order to manifest what you want (or something even better) in your material reality. Maybe you have a general idea of what you want your life to be like, but this is not enough. Maybe you are like me in the past, when one day I would want one thing, and next day I was asking for the complete opposite, going back and forth with what I wanted. If this is the case, let me tell you, you are driving the Universe nuts! Right now, I want you to take a piece of paper and write down how your perfect life would be without any limits. Everything and anything (good) is possible! Now, take a look at what you wrote and make sure that you really want that and that you do not have any opposing beliefs. Remember, clarity is very important here. Go ahead and write it all out, be clear about it all and then come back to this chapter.

Now that you have a clear idea about what your perfect life would be like, I would like to share a great yogic technique for manifesting your dreams into reality, which I practice every morning. It works for me and has worked for many of my clients and students.

Elena's Super-Fun Way to Manifest Your Perfect Life

The first step is to find your favorite "go to" song, the one that makes you want to shout for joy, that makes you feel unlimited and that brings up only good memories and happy feelings. You know, the one that makes you want to dance even in the dentist's chair!

Now, sit on the floor with your legs crossed in Easy Pose (or seated upright on a chair with both feet on the floor). Bring both of your hands into a <u>*Golden Triangle mudra*</u>*: the tips of the thumb, index and middle fingers on each hand touch to form a triangle. This is a hand position to increase your ability to manifest your heart's desires. Now, close your eyes and, as that happiness spreads through every cell of your being, listen to the song and visualize in every detail you living your perfect life with all your wishes already fulfilled. See it having manifested with ease and grace. (Don't worry about how it will happen, leave it up to the Universe to decide). While holding this mental image in your mind's eye, now bring your feelings into this experience to give it life. Imagine, how it feels to be living your perfect life. Start feeling happy, grateful and joyful for having the life of your dreams and for being so blessed, so loved and so provided for. Feel it, be excited about it, smile! When your song is over, inhale deeply through the nose, hold* *the breath for few seconds and, as you stretch your arms up, exhale and burst out laughing. Laughing after visualization serves to break any attachments we have to our desires. It is another powerful yogic secret that I use all of the time. When you are attached to your wishes and think about them all day long, it is like writing a letter to God, and never mailing it, yet still waiting for a reply. The secret is to forget about what it is you want. Letting go of thinking about your wishes is actually an act of faith. God knows what to do and hears your every thought, feeling and word.*

NOTE: Ideally you want to do this exercise for 120 days without skipping a single day. I already mentioned this before but let me get into more detail why 120. The number 120 is a powerful number and can be broken down into 40 + 40 + 40. In the first segment of 40 days you are moving your wish from the level of thought, which can be thought of as the divine plane, to the level of emotions, which can be thought of as the astral plane. In the second set of 40 days your wish is moving from the plane to the physical plane, and then for the last 40 days you are securing the manifestation of your wish on the physical plane. Therefore, I encourage you not to break the 120-day cycle, or if you do, start all over from the beginning. For some of you the manifestation of your dream might happen faster than 120 days, as it all depends on your level of consciousness and faith, but its best to play it safe and use 120 days as the magic formula. Most importantly — have fun with this activity and don't be attached! I look forward to doing my manifestation exercise each morning, because this is the time when I get to consciously co-create my reality with the Universe and listen to my favorite music. I get so happy listening to my favorite songs and seeing my life in its perfect manifestation that I raise my frequency and my whole day becomes happier and more positive after that!

Here is why it is important to listen to your favorite music while doing your visualization. Music is one of the easiest ways to evoke our feelings and feelings are the fastest way to manifest, be they positive or negative. In spirituality, feelings correspond to the lunar force, the Moon, the female principle, the Divine Mother - and everything on the Earth is affected by the Moon. It is the closest heavenly body to us. The average human body is 60% to 80% water, which means that each one of us, like the tides of the ocean, are influenced by the cycles of the Moon. Feelings are strong creative forces. Every feeling you have is a prayer. Thoughts on the other hand, correspond to the Sun or the solar force, the masculine principle and the Father. When you combine your thoughts with your feelings, the spiritual alchemy of manifestation has to happen. Just like on the physical plane when a man and a woman come together to create a new life, your thoughts mixed with your feelings create your physical reality. You need to also become aware of your emotions, which are unconscious feelings, and how powerful they are and do your best to always stay in a positive vibration. If you are too emotional, it can create a lot of difficulty in your life. You need to start being conscious about every emotion and feeling you have, so they do not control you. By bringing consciousness into anything in your life in general you are bringing healing to that matter. When you realize that you are not feeling positive, do your best to change your state of being, unless you want it to manifest into your reality. When you are having a bad day, which we all do from time to time, find a way to calm and control your emotions and raise them to a higher vibration. In the past, for me, sad emotions would call for some ice cream. Thankfully today, when I am sad I know I can always practice some rhythmic breathing, which helps the emotions to change quicker. Sometimes I will even dance around and sing along to the song I like, go for a walk, or call a good friend and it will make me feel better almost instantly. If you do happen to feel sad, you can try this breath below for a few minutes to help you transform your emotions as quickly as possible:

Elena's Favorite Breath to Heal Sadness and Depression

Position: Sit with a straight spine in Easy Pose or in a chair with a long straight spine. Arms are extended straight out in front of you, parallel to the floor. Close your right hand into a fist. Wrap your left fingers around it. The bases of the palms touch. The thumbs are close together touching and are pulled straight up. The eyes are focused on the thumbs.

Breath: Inhale slowly in one long inhale through the nose for a count of 15 seconds, counting the time in your head (do not hold the breath in). Now exhale through the nose in one long exhale for 5 seconds. Now, hold the breath out for 15 seconds. Continue with this breath pattern.

To End: Inhale deeply through the nose, hold your breath (do not hold if pregnant or have high blood pressure) and exhale. Inhale again, reach your hands to the sky, shake and exhale.

Start with 3-5 minutes and work up to 11 minutes. Build up the time slowly. In time, you can work up to holding the breath out for one full minute. However, take care not to hold the breath out so long as to make yourself dizzy or nauseous. Listen to your own body. This meditation is an antidote to depression. You will find that, properly done, it totally recharges you. It will give you the capacity to deal well with life.

5. Speak positively about your life and talk to yourself as you as if are already are the person that you want to become.

"In the beginning was the Word, and the Word was with God, and the Word was God." ~ John 1:1 (The Bible)

As I mentioned earlier, I monitor my thoughts and emotions closely these days and choose to be as positive as possible. Each thought and feeling are a form of a prayer. I do my best to do the same with my words. What you think, how you feel and what comes out of your mouth can make you or break you. Say kind and uplifting words about yourself and others. All of us here on the Earth are hungry for love. That is usually why almost all of us are addicted to something, as we try to replace that missing love with the temporary pleasure provided by addictions. If someone is pissing you off and being unkind to you, it is most likely because they need an extra amount of love. Do your best to not react and send them love and light instead. Praying for people that are not nice to you or that you do not like is not an easy task, but a necessary one, as it brings the biggest blessings into your life. You will see how those people will shift, sometimes immediately, as unconditional love heals everything and erases negative karma. Remember that every time you think, feel, speak, and act negatively, you keep demagnetizing yourself and weakening your energy field. When you choose to create your life one positive and loving thought, word, feeling and action at a time, miracles happen. Every word is God, full of divine creative energy, and you are writing the book of your life with your tongue one word at a time. One wrong word at the wrong time can ruin your entire career or relationship, and one right word at the right time can open you up to the most beautiful possibilities, and heal and comfort those who are suffering. So choose words with care and consciousness and let the Divine Love guide you as you speak so that every word that comes out of your mouth can heal and uplift you and those around you.

In spirituality, your mouth corresponds to love, and nothing but loving words should come out of your mouth. As much as you can, speak about yourself in the most positive way. Instead of complaining about yourself or your reality, pretend that you already are the person you wish to become, living your perfect life. Talk yourself into that person as much as possible, and one day, sooner or later you will be that person, guaranteed! Also, every time you hear someone talking negatively about you, do not accept it as your truth. Only people who have lost touch with their divine self can see you negatively and try to bring you down. We treat others the way we treat ourselves. Therefore, bless everyone who speaks ill of you, who criticizes you, and have compassion on them for being able to see the real you. Never let anyone define you. When you decide to walk a spiritual path of healing and personal growth, the more you change on the inside, the less and less you will attract people who will try to bring you down. When you do encounter negativity, find the self-love and strength inside yourself to say either out loud or in your mind (depending on your circumstances), "This is your limited opinion of me, based on your limited reality, and I choose to disagree with you. I choose to see myself as talented, kind, brilliant and successful in all areas of life."

Elena's Proven Way to Become Happy Through the Power of Spoken and Written Word

When I was first learning how to become positive and overcome my depression, I decided to use the word "happy" in as many sentences as I could throughout the day. I would say, "I am happy to go to the dry cleaners", "I am happy to give you a ride to the airport", "I am happy to wash the dishes." In case I would forget that I was "happy," I started to write it down everywhere in my apartment so that everywhere I turned, I would be reminded. I painted "I am Happy" on rocks and wall-hangings and placed them all around the house. I even wrote, "I AM HAPPY" on duct tape and taped it above the sink, by the trash can, on my lamp shade, you name it. That was also how I decorated the rooms in my "HappyNess Hotel" apartments I mentioned earlier in the book. Peter, being an amazing artist, started that trend by giving me 100 different hand painted cards with the word "happy" on my 31st birthday and decorating my hotel room with "I AM HAPPY" rocks. I later created a line of "I AM HAPPY" Naam Yoga socks for that reason. Over time my house became a Happy science lab, and my speech was so full of that word that it would make my friends laugh, when I would start to answer their questions with "I am happy..." yet another time.

As obsessive and silly as it sounds, it worked wonders for me. I truly manifested myself into a very happy person through saying and seeing the word "Happy" so often. I invite you as well to create your own "HappyNess Hotel" apartment and to use the word Happy in your speech as often as possible until it becomes your true inner state of mind. Make sure you are doing your morning affirmation practice, so that you can keep talking yourself into the person you wish to be!

6. Find the "Lost Word".

You have probably heard about the legend of the "lost word", an all-powerful word that was the true name of God. According to the legend, whoever possessed that knowledge would have supernatural powers. That Word was lost, and these days there are many versions on what that name could be. To me, that sacred and magic lost Word is "I AM." It is actually two words, and they are some of the most powerful ones in the world. What you put after them, you eventually become. "I Am that I Am" is the name God gave Moses when Moses asked, "Who shall I say sent me?"

I talk a lot in this book about the power of the Word. Everyone these days either knows it or at least has heard of it. I heard about this concept for many years from enlightened teachers through books, lectures, and videos. However, it was not until a few years ago that it finally dawned on me that whenever I talk negatively about myself, I am cursing myself and bringing bad luck into my life. Thankfully, the same is true for positivity. When I am kind and uplifting in my speech towards myself, I am blessing myself.

For years, even though I knew that we manifest our reality through the Word, I could not stop my internal and external diarrhea of the mouth. I was cursing. I was gossiping. I was critical and worst of all I always talked about myself in a mean way. At that time it did not look mean to me, I just thought that I was being realistic and stating the truth. "I am addicted," "I am depressed," "I am out of shape," "I am pissed off" "I am afraid," and so on were normal everyday phrases to me. These days, having a very clear awareness of how powerful everything I say is, I am careful about what I put after "I AM" throughout my day. I now continuously repeat positive "I AM" affirmations to myself, not only in the morning, but everywhere, whether I am in the shower, putting lotion on myself, at the gym doing lunges, doing laundry or running errands - I say kind things to myself mentally and out loud. It might not look like fun to some people, to be constantly training and re-programming your mind, but I know that I have years and years of negative patterns to account for and I am determined to make a loving, uplifting and positive attitude toward myself my second nature.

So there you have it — my not so secret "lost word" — "I AM". What you say after it really becomes your reality, who you are at your core essence. Choose the words that you put after "I AM" carefully and let your speech be the messenger of unconditional divine love, toward yourself and others. Life has too many unknown factors for us to add "insult to injury", so decide that no matter what happens, you are going to stay positive.

Elena's Favorite "I AM" Mantra to Open your Heart

I work extensively with this Naam mantra (a devotional prayer set to sacred sound) both personally and in my classes. When you hear this music, which is composed in accordance to advanced mathematical principles, you will probably want a copy of your own. In case you do, it can be found on the CD "Sounds of the Ether" by Dr. Joseph Michael Levry on iTunes. Listening or chanting to this mantra is a powerful way to reconnect with your true center, so that you may experience love, peace, and true joy in your life. It opens up your heart and fills you with the unconditional love of the Divine. There is nothing more healing than unconditional love, and this mantra helps you to feel that you are loved, protected and guided. Be patient and use it consistently. You will feel the light and love of the Universe almost immediately, and after repeated use your whole being will be vibrating at a higher frequency of universal love.

To work with this Naam meditation, simply sit comfortably either on the floor in Easy Pose or in a chair and place the hands over the heart. You may also enhance the experience by using the self-love mudra that I will talk about in a little bit. Chant with the meditation for 3 to 11 minutes.

7. Be Desireless.

I am sure that you have heard stories about how couples that are not able to get pregnant for a long time end up becoming pregnant after they adopt a child. In essence, once they lose their attachment to their desire, their wish manifests with ease. These babies are sometimes called "miracle babies." Even though I have never been pregnant, most of the wishes that have manifested in my life are "miracle babies". You see, when you are attached to the manifestation of your desires, pining for them all day long and wishing they were realities that act of wanting something is actually a declaration of lack. If you are telling the Universe that you are lacking, it will reflect back to you with even more lack. In other words, when you want something, what you are doing is stating to the Universe that you do not have it; and the universe, responding to your programming, brings you more of that which you do not have. Sounds crazy, right? When you know what you want and you see your wish clearly in your mind's eye, the secret to manifesting it is to take on a feeling inside as you already have it. If you already have it, why would you desire it? Talk to yourself and feel as if you already have what you want. The magic of alchemy begins when you assume the mental and emotional attitude of your wish being fulfilled. Acting as if you already have your wish sets into motion a sequence of events that crystallizes your desire into physical reality. Some people call this faith. Your job during the three minute music visualization I described earlier is to see and be clear about your wish, feel the happiness of receiving it, and then go about your day and live like your desire is already your reality and you actually do not desire it at all. Basically you need to forget about your visualization all together. It is those wishes that we really want that we all too often have trouble relaxing about and therefore receiving. We constantly think about them and talk about them, or mostly about the lack of them. We really want them and this is exactly why they do not come into our life with the same ease as the little things we wish for and instantly forget about.

Let me share a "miracle baby" story from a 2015 New Year's Eve Celebration that I went to in Los Angeles. I was in a room filled with hundreds of people at Naam Yoga LA and we were waiting for Dr. Levry to come into the room and start the New Year's Meditation. Earlier I had been at a nearby hotel where the staff was preparing many balloons and placing them in the lobby. Once I was at the Center and we started to meditate, I began to imagine how I would decorate my own hotel one day. "I would really like the ceiling to be full of stars," I thought. My next thought was: "How would I put the stars on the ceiling, it is so high, and what would those stars be made out of?" I didn't give that desire more than few seconds total, switching to another train of thought and forgetting all about the stars. This was at about 11PM. Three hours into the celebration (it was an all-night event), my friend Nikky met up with us. She walked over to where I was sitting and said, "Happy New Year buddy! I got you something. I was in the toy store shopping for my little nephew, and I got both of you this." She gave me a box that said, "Star making machine!" No joke. It was a machine that makes stars out of light and projects them onto the ceiling. It took only three hours for a most random but very clear thought mixed with positive emotions to manifest in the physical plane. So there you have it, something that we don't care that much about can manifest super-fast! Still, the 120-day formula discussed earlier is very powerful for those things that take a little more time. Just remember to act and feel throughout your day like you have already "have your baby". Do not express worry, fear, or attachment to how and when your wish will become a reality. Maybe you will get so good at it that you will not need to complete the entire 120-days. I hope so! Just work with it. Wish it, see it, feel it, live it. Be it. Become desireless.

Work with this concept until it becomes your second nature. I sometime joke that my desire is to be desireless. I love living in the land of no desire as much as possible throughout the day and instead feeling gratitude for everything. If you want to be attached to anything in this life, be attached to God. Everything and everyone else is not permanent and it all shall pass. Plus you can't take anything with you when you are dead. What counts the most when you are dead is how many hearts you have opened and how many people you have helped. Go out into the world every day knowing that all of your wishes have already manifested. Soon enough you will be the proud and happy parent of your "miracle babies".

Elena's Favorite Example of How to Become Desireless: Wear the Dress!

Let's say you want a beautiful red dress, but you don't have any money to buy the particular red dress of your dreams. This is what you do. Get another dress out of your closet, put it on and pretend that it IS the red dress that you want! Believe in your heart that you are already wearing your red dress instead of just wishing for it. As you are walking around with the dress on, convince yourself that you are wearing that gorgeous red dress, and therefore there is no need to desire it. You are already wearing it! You can bring all five senses into this practice. See the red dress fitting you beautiful-ly. Feel the softness and smell the newness of the fabric. Hear the sound that the dress makes as you sashay around and hear your friends telling you how good you look in that dress! You can even taste the beautiful dinner that you are having while out on the town in your beautiful red dress! Before you know it, if you continue to stay in this state of feeling that the dress you pulled out of the closet is the real red dress, it will manifest in your physical reality for everyone else to admire it also. The same method applies for your other desires as well. Make yourself believe that you already have what you want, and when you want nothing you will have everything!

8. Say 'NO!' to gossip and criticism. Do not complain and stay away from people who do.

I try as much as possible to stay away from pessimistic people, those who gossip and are life's chronic complainers. I believe that you should love everyone unconditionally and wish everyone well, yet choose only the company of positive and uplifting people. Basically, I run away from anyone these days who even closely reminds me of myself a few years ago. I ask God to bless them and then make a gracious exit.

On the occasion that I do judge someone in my mind, I immediately change the thought into a positive one and send that person a blessing. I do my best to keep my mind clean by not allowing gossip and anything negative, pessimistic, violent or mean to penetrate it. Everything that we say, hear and see becomes part of what mystics call the Akashic record, or the "Book of Life," and it cannot be erased, only atoned for. Everything we experience, see, hear and say affects our energy field in a positive or negative way. Gossiping is like digging a grave with your own teeth. When you gossip or talk negatively about a person, a change of energy happens that does not work in your favor and you being to loose your light. The same rule applies to simply being in the company of a gossiper and listening to him or her in person or on TV. So choose the company of positive people, choose positive programming when you watch TV, read uplifting books and articles and focus on good things in life. When you choose to focus on that which is good and ignore that which is bad, when your speech is positive and uplifting, when you act with kindness towards yourself and others, the universe blesses you with more and more light and happiness in your life. Light is akin to an invisible spiritual "bank account," remember? You want to have it. The more light you have in your aura, the luckier you are and the more blessings and positive experiences can enter your life. Every time you speak ill of another person, you demagnetize your aura and decrease your light. Should you hear someone gossip about or criticize others, either change the topic of conversation or leave the room.

Elena's Favorite way to Magnetize the Aura

The powerful healing sound THO is for your thyroid gland, throat chakra and to give you a bright, strong and beautiful aura (pronounced "ZO" like in "Go"). Vibrating THO will also give you youth and mental power.

Posture/Movement: Sit on the floor with legs crossed in Easy Pose or on a chair with your feet on the floor.

Mudra: Hands by your shoulders, palms open and facing forward, as if you are giving an oath with both hands. This mudra helps build light in the energy field and makes one very likable.

Breath: Inhale deeply, hold the breath for a second and on the exhale chant the word: "ZZZZZOOOOOOOOOOOO", using the entire breath for a single repetition. Repeat three, seven times or eleven times total. Helpful tip:

Spend several seconds on the "Z", feeling the sound vibrate inside of the mouth and then move into "O" for the rest of the breath.

To End: Inhale, briefly suspend the breath and then exhale.

9. Meditation and Breathwork.

I attribute a large part of my healing from my mental and emotional challenges to the specific breath work and meditations presented by Naam Yoga. I have been doing them every day, twice a day, for a number of years now. Nobody in their right mind is going to spend that much time doing something that doesn't work! Through breathwork and meditation we can learn to control our mind, so it eventually becomes our puppy, and not our master. Remember what I said earlier that the mind always follows the breath, and if you know how to breathe, you can control your mind and in turn control your emotions and feelings? You can think of Naam meditation as the "fast-forward" method of helping the mind to clear out negative chatter, self-sabotaging beliefs, old programming, destructive patterns and any other mental garbage you may be hanging on-to. Again, no one can clean your mind but you, and you have all the tools you need right under your nose.

When I skip a day or two of meditation, I notice a huge difference in the quality of my thoughts and feelings. I become critical, reactive, depressed and pessimistic which as you know, are the very patterns we are changing with the help of this book. Meditation is like a mental workout. Some people are born naturally slim and picture perfect, but the rest of us need to work out and eat well in order to maintain a lean, toned body. Like many others, when I put off exercising out and give into bad food choices, my body changes and my waist-line expands and the only thing I want expanding these days is my aura and my consciousness. The same thing goes for meditation and breath-work. Some of us were born naturally positive, brought up in a supportive, nurturing, and loving environments, and are one hundred percent optimistic, glass half-full kind of people all of the time. Most of us, however, need to put forth some effort and practice a discipline to refine on our mind and mental attitude, in order to be happy, centered and balanced, and to lead a positive, blissful life.

I invite you to give it a try — even just three to eleven minutes a day of Naam meditation and breath-work will help you to experience less anger, feel more centered and think more positively. The most favorable times to do your practice are from 4 -7 AM (also known as the "ambrosial hours") and or from 4 -7 PM. Another great time to meditate is right before you go to sleep. Still, you can meditate any time of day and get great results. If possible, I highly recommend meditating at the same time everyday.

Elena's Favorite Breath Exercise for Personal Magnetism and Attracting Your Soulmate

This breath was taught to me by Dr. Levry a few years ago, and is one of the most powerful breath techniques ever known. Working with it on a regular basis will make you magnetic, healthy and help you manifest your desires. It is also known to help you attract your soul mate! So get excited if you are looking for one, because even if your soul mate is living in China right now, he/she will be making their way to you!

<u>Position:</u> Sit in an Easy Pose with your spine straight, hands in Gyan mudra on your knees, tips of thumbs to the tips of your index fingers. This mudra expands consciousness, promotes self-wisdom and helps break through challenges. Gyan mudra works on your lung meridian. Make sure your spine is straight, crown of your head reaching to the sky and chin slightly tucked in.

<u>Breath:</u> First let's go back to the prayer of Love, Peace and Light I talk in chapter 11. It can also be found on Rootlight CD Pranic Power should you like to listen to it. It would be good for you to memorize it eventually, in the beginning you can keep the book open on the prayer as you do this breath. Start inhaling slowly while mentally vibrating the "Love" portion of the prayer. As you exhale slowly mentally vibrate both the "Peace" and "Light" portions of the prayer for the entire long and deep exhale. As you

can gather, the ratio of inhale to exhale is 1:2. You are exhaling twice as long as you are inhaling. With regular practice this yogic breath increases lung capacity, brings more oxygen supply to the body, and helps eliminate toxins. Your metabolism and overall health will improve and your stress level will be reduced. This breath makes your aura very strong, and eventually you will attract your heart's desires. It is a very powerful technique that yogis know and use for manifestation.

Tip: If this breath exercise seems too difficult at first, you can simply start by inhaling to the count of 10 and exhaling to the count of 20. Still too hard? Try inhaling for 5 seconds and exhaling for 10 seconds. Overtime begin to increase the times and include the mental recitation of the prayer.

To End: Inhale deeply and bring the hands up overhead. Hold your breath briefly, visualize yourself in bright light, see your desire as your reality, then burst out laughing as you shake your arms vigorously to distribute the energy throughout your entire body.

10. Know how to get yourself out of a funk.

When things feel very bleak in my life, it is usually during those times when I stop my daily Naam meditation practice. In this case, my negative mind takes over and freaks out over any and every situation or person and I usually start feeling sorry for myself and depressed about my life. The good news is that this helps me understand just how powerful meditation is and how vital it is to being happy and peaceful. Meditation and breath-work calm the mind and make it our puppy. Without meditation, we are susceptible to becoming slaves of our mind, and everything seems much more catastrophic than it really is.

Our state of mind and our thoughts shape our emotions and attitude toward life. When you can remain positive in a negative situation, you disarm that situation's capacity to harm you and shift it into a positive outcome. When you are positive in a positive situation you become limitless! The mind, by virtue of its capacity to choose our thoughts and feelings, shapes our reality. You can live in Paradise or Hell. It is your choice.

Every day we wake up and the universe gives us another day, full of beautiful new energy and unlimited possibilities. Most of us have no access to this limitless bounty because we have stacked bricks of anger, fear, past memories and hurt feelings so high all around us that it is completely out of our reach. As we said earlier, insanity is practicing the same thing over and over again and expecting different results. Many of us have made a practice of this for so long, that we are completely unaware of the snare we have set for ourselves.

So when I feel like I am in a funk, when my mind starts going cuckoo, when I feel like I am doomed and that I should go
live in a car or become homeless because I will never be successful, and that there is no hope for me, I know now that this
is my soul calling out to me for the lifeline of my Naam meditations and breathwork. Rhythmic breath is the fastest way to
shift your emotions from negative to positive. It only takes
about three minutes to feel a difference. I am usually able to re-
verse my "funk" rather fast now because I can recognize that
my salvation is in my own hands and under my nose. No one
will come and rescue me, or give me what I want on a silver
platter when I am hiding in my bedroom with a pint of ice
cream, crying and feeling sorry for myself. Only I can save me
and create the life of my dreams, with meditation, mantra,
breath-work and with one positive thought, word, feeling, attitude and action at a time.

What else gets me out of a funk besides meditation? Well,
for starters, my gratitude list. I know this might sound cliché to
some. The repeated mention of it has perhaps diluted its reputation, but when my mood is really low, and nothing in my life
seems to be going the way I want it to — making a gratitude
list, mentally or on paper, has saved me many times over. When
I am able to clearly see how many blessings there are in my life
and how much bigger other people's problems actually might

be, I want to kick myself in the butt and never feel sad again about all those "challenges" I go through, like that my boyfriend broke up with me, my friend and I are not getting along, and so on and forth, as they are just a small tiny bump on the road. People deal with much bigger issues and I am blessed to only have little hiccups that are really insignificant. If you happen to be faced with any challenges right now, know that there is nothing that you cannot overcome, big or small. But no matter how small or serious your problem is — think of one thing you are grateful for, or one person you are grateful for. Put this person or thing on your gratitude list and focus on it at any time when your mind wants you to believe that everything is "horrible", "dark" or "hopeless."

I know that I am extremely blessed to be alive and to be able to move and walk, and that many people in the world do not have this ability. To remind myself of this, I go for a walk on the beach and it always cheers me up. Last, but not least, when I am down I like to watch funny videos, movies or sitcoms and call a best friend.

Below is a space for you to write down three things that you can fall back on right away when you start feeling negative or pessimistic about yourself. Know what they are and force yourself to refer to this list and do the things that get you out of your funk. If you haven't done it yet, create a gratitude list that includes everything that you are grateful for. Make sure you list even the smallest blessings in your life, like a chance to wake up in the morning for a fresh new start, as it is not a guarantee. When you feel like complaining about your life, refer to your list and do your best to shift your perspective and start remembering how blessed you truly are.

Three things I can do get myself out of a funk:

1._____

2._____

3._____

Elena's Favorite Funk-Buster Breathing Technique

Breath of Glow is a powerful exercise I discovered while learning Naam Yoga that can change your mood in a very short amount of time. Yogis call it "The King of all breaths." Why does it work? It significantly increases the amount of oxygen flow to the brain. It helps remove negativity from the aura, making it brighter and leaves one feeling blissful and relaxed.

Posture: Sit comfortably in Easy Pose on in a chair with a straight spine.

Mudra: Touch the thumb tips to the tips of the ring and pinky fingers (Silver Triangle mudra). This mudra will build your life-force and takes care of many things within the body.

Breath: This breath emphasizes exhaling. Imagine that there is a candle in front of you that you can only blow out with your nose. As you exhale through your nose to blow the candle out, gently pull the navel in toward the spine. Repeat this over and over, blowing out through the nose as you pull the navel in. The inhale, or filling back up of the lungs, will happen naturally in between the exhales. This is a rhythmic breath. You are exhaling about one exhale per second. Dr. Levry has created several beautiful tracks of music specifically for Naam Yoga practitioners to use while doing Breath of Glow. You might wish to try one of the following CDs: Kabbalah for Healing (track five) or Naam Lounge. You can continue with the breath for 3-10 minutes.

To End: Inhale, briefly suspend the breath, close your eyes, see the light around you expanding and then exhale.

11. Love Yourself Unconditionally.

"There are two basic motivating forces: fear and love. When we are afraid, we pull back from life. When we are in love, we open to all that life has to offer with passion, excitement, and acceptance. We need to learn to love ourselves first, in all our glory and our imperfections. If we cannot love ourselves, we cannot fully open to our ability to love others or our potential to create. Evolution and all hopes for a better world rest in the fearlessness and open-hearted vision of people who embrace life." ~ John Lennon

Every morning in my meditations, I ask God to help me love myself unconditionally that day, to make healthy loving choices toward my body and spirit, to be watchful of my ego and to neutralize my body of pain. For those of you who do not know what "body of pain" is, it refers to the self-destructive behaviors we humans participate in and may manifest in many ways such as: jealousy, anger, possessiveness, stubbornness, procrastination, a closed-heart, over self-indulgence, refusing to forgive others and the list goes on and on. Actually, when it comes to the body of pain, I highly recommend that everyone read either "The Divine Doctor" or "Lifting the Veil" by Dr. Joseph Michael Levry. These books will take you on an in-depth journey of your personal planetary make-up according to your day of birth, your virtues and your vices and how to neutralize your specific body of pain so that more blessings can flow into your life.

Nothing good comes out of a love relationship where one or both partners are lacking a strong and healthy sense of self-love. I was a complete stranger to the concept of self-love until just a few years ago. I was literally swimming in my body of pain! I didn't know that self-love even existed! Think of the masses when they still thought the world was flat! I now know that it is possible to love yourself in a way that is not selfish, but nourishing, caring and unconditional. It is no surprise that my relationship with Tom suffered and crumbled, just like all of my other relationships before him. When I moved to LA, I was so excited about getting over him, but it was harder than I thought, as you already know. The truth is, and I learned this through Divine Spiritual Wisdom, every sexual partner that you have leaves an imprint in your aura. Women are especially sensitive to this imprint for the simple reason that a woman's heart is connected with her uterus and a man's is not, therefore he is not as badly affected should the relationship be broken. This explains why so often it is harder for a woman to move on than it is for a man. Furthermore, the more sexual partners a woman has, the weaker her energy field and vitality become, making her look older faster and making her vulnerable to more unlucky circumstances. The good news is, if you are a man or a woman desiring to move on as quickly as possible from a "failed" love relationship, you can work with the Naam meditation on Rootlight's "Blissful Spirit" CD called "Ganputi Mantra" as it washes the aura clean when practiced faithfully.

I invite you to create a ritual, just like brushing your teeth, to "polish" your self-love. Looking for love outside of yourself to fulfill you will often lead to suffering. We often think we will find the love we are looking for by attaching to another human. If you are going to be attached to anything, attach yourself to God. God, or whatever you call the all-pervading presence, is the source of all love and love is the fabric of the universe. Self-love, when properly cultivated, is something that no one can take away from you.

Self-love is the beginning of self-healing. Self-love is not selfish. If you want to be happy, you need to know how to really love yourself, so you can start loving others and loving God and all sacred teachings. When you love yourself, you give permission to others to love you. When you love yourself you find God. When you find God, you find yourself.

Elena's Favorite Way to Cultivate Self-Love

I would like to share a meditation with you that is extremely heart-opening. If you have no idea how to go about loving yourself, dive into this meditation as soon as possible! Don't blame me if your whole world opens up and your entire life changes!

Position: Sit either in Easy Pose or in a chair with the feet on the floor and keep a long straight spine.

Meditation: Bring your hands into the mudra for self-love. Begin by bringing the palms together and interlacing the fingers. Your fingers are the remote controls of your life. Then, extend the thumbs so that the thumb tips touch each other. Do the same thing with the index fingers and the pinky fingers-extend them straight up so that the tips of the fingers touch. The base of the palms are open. Place this mudra in front of the heart (not touching the body) with the elbows relaxed at the sides. Close your eyes and go within. Chant along with mantra "I Am", which can be found on the Rootlight CD "Sounds of the Ether".

To End: Inhale deeply, hold your breath for a few seconds, visualize yourself in beautiful pink light (the color of love), and exhale.

12. Take responsibility for raising your vibration — don't blame others for your life circumstances.

I spent a large part of my life with a victim mentality, "Oh, poor me, everything is happening to me, everyone is so mean to me, etc..." were my normal every day thoughts. I blamed everyone for my misery and was constantly complaining. Until one day I realized that I am the Goodness of God and God is within me. It stands to reason then, if God is within me, it makes me the co-creator of my own life, consciously or unconsciously. My thoughts, my words and my feelings manifest my reality. What I do today forms my future, and today is the result of how I thought, felt, spoke and acted in the past. Let's put it this way, if you think your life sucks it's because you created it! This realization made me understand that if I want to live a happier life, I had to raise my consciousness and become a positive co-creator, as opposed to being a victim.

The circumstances of our lives are the result of our own consciousness. Any problem that you have in your life is just an effect and is rooted in negative patterns and beliefs, which are the causes, conscious or unconscious. In order to rise above the clouds of problems and suffering, we have to raise our consciousness and rid the mind of negative thought patterns. We can do this by working with mantra, meditation, breath-work, reading spiritual books and using positive affirmations.

Elena's Favorite Mantra to Raise your Vibration

I want to share a powerful Naam meditation with you that works on the brain in a very specific and powerful way to help you elevate your state of being. Many people are aware that inside of the brain are the pituitary and pineal glands, but they don't know a science for getting these glands to wake up, resonate and talk to each other so as to benefit the entire body. These glands are known as the "master glands" and their proper functioning can determine our mood, our decision making capacity, the strength of our intuition and the health of our body. Have you ever went to a doctor who said, "Go home and fix your master glands?" I don't think so. I never have. When we are young, the pituitary and pineal glands communicate perfectly, but as we reach puberty, the transformation that takes place in our hormones can offset the perfect functioning of these glands, which also explains why many teenagers and young adults go through trying times and can often be rebellious. When you work with the following sacred sound, which is AUM - the universal name of the Creator and the key to the true knowledge of self — you are telling your master glands, "Wake up! Do your job!" When this happens, I know you will benefit from it as much as I have. Here is how you can work with this sound:

Position: Sit either in Easy Pose or in a chair with the feet on the floor and keep a long straight spine.

Mudra: Create fists with both of your hands. Place them in the area between your eyebrows, or third eye, stacked on top of each other, with right fist being on top of the left.

Mantra: Chant AUM. Make every AUM devotional and imagine that as you are chanting it, all your problems are being melted away. If you wish to chant along to the Aum Mantra recorded on Rootlight CD called "Sacred Aum", you can find it on iTunes. Chant this mantra for 3 minutes or longer if desired.

End: Inhale deeply, hold your breath for a few seconds, visualize yourself in beautiful light, feel peaceful and as if all your problems have been taken care of and exhale.

13. Elena's Favorite Energy Healing System in the World

I already mentioned the Harmonyum Healing System before in this book. I have been receiving Harmonyum Healing sessions for years now and using it with hundreds of clients. It is such an amazing healing system that it deserves to be given a little bit more explanation. Like many others, I swear by the Harmonyum Healing. I first started receiving it in NYC without much understanding of how powerful it is. When I first learned about it, I would go get one once a week just because it felt so nice and served as the most beautiful thing that I could possibly look forward to after a drama-filled week. For eight years, I suffered from severe lower back and neck pain due to four herniated discs that I developed as a result of serious car accidents. I was experiencing so much pain that I sought out every kind of therapy, laser, massage, ultrasound, you name it, and yet I was never able to sit for more than two hours in a car or a plane without an excruciating pain. Due to the fact that my doctors told me that I would have to deal with that pain for the rest of my life, I developed the mentality that my pain would last forever. About seven months after receiving Harmonyum, I suddenly realized that the back and neck pain had disappeared. I couldn't notice a single trace of it in my body.

Around this same time, my relationship with Tom was dissolving and I decided to move to LA. It was there that I decided to find out more about what makes Harmonyum so effective and so I took my first Harmonyum Healing Training, which lasted for four days. During the training I felt so many emotions being cleared out of me, at such a fast pace. As they say, you have to heal yourself first before you can heal others. I think that is exactly what was happening. Something else that stood out were the words of Dr. Levry: "If you hate your job, don't like your boyfriend, but you do not wish your life to change, then you shouldn't come anywhere near a Harmonyum session, as it will cleanse everything from your life that is not of your highest good." Then it dawned on me, that it was while I was receiving regular Harmonyum treatments that my relationship with Tom took a course for the worse. You see, many of us are unhappy with many aspects of our lives, but we never change because we are in our comfort zone. I was in my comfort zone of abundance and luxury, and I didn't want to leave that life. Then, all of a sudden, it was gone. Harmonyum brought me to a place where I could no longer live a lie.

Harmonyum healing is the most powerful healing system I have ever encountered and as you know I tried many different things. Harmonym is a transcendental healing system that helps to cleanse the body of trauma and negative patterns. What we cannot face ourselves, or what might take us decades to face, Harmonyum allows us to face in several days or several weeks. Most people think that the root of disease and unhappiness lies in the physical body when it actually starts in our mental body or the way that we think and speak. A mind that is pessimistic and believes the worst sends discordant vibrations to the physical body that eventually manifests as disease. In order to heal your body you need to heal your mind. I now simply can't imagine my life without Harmonyum.

I have clients from all walks of life that benefit tremendously from receiving Harmonyum. Few years ago I gave a Harmonyum to a legendary Broadway dancer and director who injured his back just a day before his performance. After receiving only one Harmonyum, he was able to perform the next day to a sold out show. I have another client who is 11 years old with a bright future in modeling and acting who has struggled with OCD for years. After only seven sessions her symptoms reduced significantly and she is able to function in her day-to-day life with much more ease and comfort. I could give you many other examples.

Harmonyum, along with Naam Yoga, is a big reason I was able to overcome depression, binge eating, OCD and was able to develop a loving relationship with myself and with my family. Thanks to both healing practices, I was able to shed so much of my darkness and open up more and more to the most beautiful person that I never knew existed. There are now thousands of Harmonyum practitioners and Naam Yogis all over the world. You are very welcome to come to Santa Monica, or other cities where Harmonyum training is offered and take the training yourself. It is a great way to learn how to start serving others. I think it would be great if there were a Harmonyum practitioner in every household.

I find that in life, when I really want something, if it is aligned with the will of God, it manifests easily. When I was just seventeen years old, living in Belarus, without a penny to my name, and just a strong desire to come to the U.S., I won a scholarship to go to high school in Texas for a year. Later I was able to get a scholarship to a private college in the US. I am telling you this in order to encourage you to follow your desires and if Harmonyum sounds like something that you want or need, you should find a way to do so no matter where you are in the world. You might even become the first person in your country or your state to become a Harmonyum practitioner.

14. Be Yourself - that is all that you can be.

"You don't need anybody to tell you who you are or what you are. You are what you are!" "I'm not going to change the way I look or the way I feel to conform to anything. I've always been a freak. So I've been a freak all my life and I have to live with that, you know. I'm one of those people."
~ John Lennon

"Have the courage to be yourself. Trouble comes when you are looking for validation and approval." ~ Dr. Joseph Michael Levry

For many years I thought that some people were destined to be happy and some to be miserable and that there was virtually no hope for the latter. Naturally, I was a self-assigned member of the miserable category. Thank God that these days my consciousness has expanded and I am strongly convinced that we are all born to be happy and to shine our beauty and light into the world. No exceptions. There is no "lucky us" versus the rest of the world. We all are here for a specific and unique purpose. No one is here by accident. There is no such thing as junk DNA. No one is here to be miserable and to have a hard life. Yet we can make the journey out of illusion and misfortune when we commit to discovering who we are and once there, accept and unconditionally love ourselves. Very often we think that we need to be "important", successful financially, physically attractive, funny, or whatever else we come up with to be accepted by others and get their approval. We strive for things like nice cars, designer clothes, perfect bodies and big homes hoping to fill our inner voids with external validation. For years, I only felt beautiful in expensive clothes and boy, did I think I was something special when I would pull out my platinum Amex card. In college I had zero friends because I felt like I did not fit in into a private school. Rich kids with nice clothes and fancy cars surrounded me. I felt ashamed that I was from Belarus and overexerted myself pretending to be American, thinking that it must be cooler to be an American than a Belarusian. Now I know that all you need to be is to be yourself. Who are YOU? What makes you unique? Where did you come from? What are your roots? You need to know where you are coming from in order to know where you are going. If divine intelligence made you to be born in India or China or wherever else — there must be a reason for it. You have to appreciate the fact that you are different from anyone else in this world. Don't try to copy someone else, a celebrity or another person that you know — you can never be them. All you can do is be the best version of you and in turn, no one can copy you. The outstanding people of our times found the courage to be themselves, and if it was necessary, to go against what was expected of them by their family, partners, teachers and society. They expressed their true nature, instead of trying to impress others. When you are connected to your inner truth, when you no longer come from a place of ego, you do not care anymore whether or not others approve of you and your life. When you know who you are, you free up limitless reservoirs of energy to do what makes you truly happy, and when this happens, life becomes magical. You create beautiful songs, films, books and other things that touch people's lives. You find your passion in whatever field your talents are in, and because it comes from your heart, you are sure to contribute to the energy that makes this world a better place. We are all born with a light in us. Once you get in touch with this light, you will make a huge difference and have a huge impact on others.

I only became proud of who I am and where I came from in the last few years. When I first moved to America, I was so ashamed of being a "poor girl" from Belarus. Even when I lived with Tom and had lots of money and made significant advances in my career, I still felt inadequate. I was still thinking that Tom's friends, who were all super successful, were somehow better, cooler, or smarter than me, just because they grew up in America. I wasted so much energy just trying to fit in with them. I thought of myself as less of a person than his upper-class American friends. It took me many years to get to the place of being proud of my roots, but I am finally grateful for my upbringing. I am grateful for experiencing hardships, lack and scarcity growing up, because now I feel like there is no place in the world where I would not be able to survive. I once saw a funny clip on YouTube called: "Russians are the scariest white people", where a comedian told the audience that if he ever felt like he was in danger of being mugged he would successfully defend himself by faking a Russian accent. I couldn't help but agree with his strategy! The truth is that Soviet block people have endured untold hardships and because of that they are very tough, maybe even downright scary. Still, I am grateful for the inner strength that my country gave me. I love being Belarusian now. I love mashed potatoes, beets and borscht! I now declare openly that I do not care for a peanut butter and jelly sandwich, and an Oreo cookie dunked in milk does not look appetizing to me. I am proud to be Canadian- American – Belarusian, but mostly proud to be a citizen of a universe where we are all interconnected. I would like you to take a moment and write down below at least three things that you too can be proud and grateful for, based on your roots and your upbringing, and that make you your unique self:

1._____

2._____

3._____

15. To become truly happy you need to "uncondition" yourself.

"There's no separation. We're all one. "Give peace a chance," not "Shoot people for peace." "All you need is love." I believe it. It's damn hard, but I absolutely believe it." " If someone thinks that love and peace is a cliché that must have been left behind in the Sixties, that's his problem. Love and peace are eternal." ~ John Lennon

When I say "un-condition" yourself, what I am really asking you to do is become universal. It is time for us all to think beyond the conditioning of society, religion, culture, race, upbringing and environment so that we can be happier, and bring love, peace and happiness into the world on a grand scale. Our world needs a lot of love and a lot of peace and a lot of joy. This is possible when we all think that we are "One" versus "us against them". While it is good to know where you are coming from, it is now time to think bigger than "I am Canadian", "I am American", "I am Belarusian", "I am white", "I am black", "I am Christian", "I am Jewish", etc. The truth is that there is no separation. We all have red blood and white bones. Show me somebody who has green blood and purple polka-dotted bones. We are all individual units of consciousness of a greater collective body and the more we serve each other, the stronger our collective body will become. To get there we all need to open our hearts to divine love and to our true universal nature. The purpose of spirituality is to open your heart and then to find your true note in universal harmony. When you think and act each day not from the illusion of separation, but with a perspective of the unity of all beings, when you focus on what you have in common with others rather than your differences, you become a driving force for change on the planet. You join the new wave of people who, like Gandhi, know that "an eye for an eye makes the whole world blind". A world where love, peace and light are the ruling energies is quickly emerging and the faster you align yourself with these truths, the easier it will be for everyone. So come on — let's get "unconditioned"!

Elena's Favorite Meditation for Re-patterning Our Consciousness

I would like to share a powerful Naam meditation with you that serves as a very effective tool in unveiling our true spiritual being. The mantra used in this meditation is "Hari Om" and later in the CD the mantra switches to "I am I am". It is said that working with the mantra Hari Om can lead us to self-realization and free us from ignorance and negative thinking. This mantra can be found on the Rootlight CD Celestial Naam. I highly recommend it. Here is how to do this meditation:

Position: Sit either in Easy Pose or in a chair with the feet on the floor and keep a long straight spine.

Practice: Place the hands on the heart, close your eyes and go deep inside. Begin to chant the mantra "Hari Om" along with the CD. After several minutes into it, chant "I am I am". You can begin by doing the meditation anywhere from 3-11 minutes.

End: _Take a deep inhale, briefly suspend the breath, see yourself in light, and then exhale._

If possible, try to do this meditation every day at the same time for maximum results.

16. Your Word Should be as Good as Gold

"All I want is the truth. Just give me some truth" ~ John Lennon

"Naam" means "Word". When we do Naam meditations we are working with the power of the word. What I learned from the very beginning of my spiritual journey was that the more I meant what I said, the more I honored every word that came out of my mouth and the more the Universe honored me in return. Your word has to be as good as gold. My grandfather used to say this to me all of the time, but it was not until I was in my thirties that I fully grasped and appreciated this principle. Be honest and conscious of how you use your word and don't over-promise when you cannot deliver. When you give your word to someone, you have to do your very best to keep it. Keeping your word causes many blessings to flow into your life. Your name will speak for itself and it will become your brand.

Think of honesty as a super-fun game where you never need to remember what you said and to whom, as you always say the truth (in a diplomatic, gentle way of course). As the old saying goes, "The good thing about telling the truth is that you can tell it over and over again." For me, those days of little white lies are over. If, let's say, I don't want to go to a party, I simply say: "Thank you for the invitation, but I cannot make it." What I would do in the past was say: "Thank you so much, I would love to come, but I have family visiting from out of town." For some reason, I always felt like I had to explain myself and give a "valid" reason why I couldn't do something, like my feelings and desires alone were not good enough. I feel so liberated now, knowing that the only thing that matters is being true to myself and honoring how I feel.

When you are always honest and respectful of your words, they become very powerful and full of energy. So as you value and practice genuine honesty you will eventually become the active co-creator of your reality, where everything you say manifests on the physical plane effortlessly and almost immediately (in accordance with divine time of course). You will start finding yourself in the right place at the right time more and more often, and all of the people who are here to help you on your path will be drawn to you. It's that easy. When you mean everything you say, it makes it easy for others to be around you.

When you practice honesty, it takes the guessing game out of your communication with others. They know that when you say you would love to come to their party, you really mean it. You are not just saying it because you can't come up with a good excuse. Surprisingly enough, I find myself less and less in situations where I feel the need to justify myself. Most of the people that are in my life now are open to clear and respectful communication. When I have something unpleasant that I can't avoid being discussed, I do my best to approach the person and the situation with love, and I always say a prayer before the conversation, asking God to speak through me. When you come from a place of love and appreciation for another person, even though the topic you have to discuss might be heavy, somehow the words that come out of your mouth are constructive and it's easy to find a mutually beneficial solution. Sometimes I hear people, especially in the business or corporate world, say that you need to be able to bend the truth, that it is okay to tell a few white lies here and there and kiss your boss's behind at times. I can relate to this, as I was part of the corporate world for many years, and being in sales I had to (or I thought I had to) bend the truth at times with my customers. I used to have no problem with it back then. I thought, "Oh, it's just a small lie, I'm not doing any harm to anyone." I did not realize at that time that there really is no difference between a big lie and a small lie.

The act of lying still chips away from your character. I used to be the ultimate people pleaser and I would say things that I thought would make people like me more, or at least not get mad at me, or get me the sale that I needed to meet my monthly goals. I was a successful sales representative, but I wasn't a happy person. I ended up getting myself into a lot of emotional trouble by being dishonest. This was my favorite "game" to play — I would lie, feel terrible, get overwhelmed with guilt and then binge on sugar to numb the emotional pain. At times, I ended up going back and confessing to people that I had lied to and I would end up hurting inside and feeling guilty even more, as I had now become a source of pain for others. This went on and on until I realized that I only have to be a self-pleaser and stop looking for approval of others, and that I must be honest, at all times and with everyone. It was hard to break the habit of lying and people pleasing. I was so good at both for so many years! To help me in the process I created affirmations such as, "The only person I need to please is myself. I am the most honest person I know. I speak my truth with grace and kindness." I would repeat them on a daily basis and over time they became my reality. Later I "upgraded" my affirmations to, "I attract honest people in my life who honor and respect themselves as well as myself and who value their word." Again, because your thoughts and words become your reality, these affirmations beame my reality. Most of my closest friends and people I see every day value the word and its powerful creative potential. I am not writing this with the assumption that you tell white lies like I did. However, if there are some moments where you know what you are saying is not exactly true, take a deeper look inside. When we lie to others, it also gives us permission to lie to ourselves. So when you are saying, "Tomorrow I will start exercising and eating healthy," do you really mean it — and more importantly — do you trust your own word? Do your best to keep all of the promises you make to yourself and others. Be conscious of your words. Speak in a way that anybody listening to you in the entire world could benefit and then see how much easier and happier your life is.

Elena's Honesty Check

Take a moment today and think about what areas of your life you could be more honest with yourself in. If you know you have some weak spots about being honest, ask why it is so, what belief or habit makes you act this way? Take action if you see any weak areas. You don't have to transform overnight. Make one small improvement each day. Through my spiritual journey I became conscious enough to understand that I used to lie a lot. Actually, I learned this behavior from adults when I was a child and I simply thought that it was a way of life. Sometimes, I was scared to tell

150

the truth to my parents for fear of being punished. These unhealthy behaviors continued into my adult years. It took me some time to become conscious and aware of this tendency and to successfully change it. You too can start today and figure out where the change needs to happen. Becoming conscious of your habits is half of the battle!

17. Have Faith in the Universe.

"If being an egomaniac means I believe in what I do and in my art or music, then in that respect you can call me that... I believe in what I do, and I'll say it." "There's nothing you can do that can't be done....." ~ John Lennon

Throughout the years of dealing with depression, an eating disorder and other challenges, I was not sure how I was ever going to get better, so I just kept asking God to help me. I was praying for Him to show me how to stop binging, stop feeling down on myself and stop thinking that I was unworthy of anything good. I thought I was the world's biggest loser. I wanted to change and heal myself so much. I used to look for the answer how to get there by going to church every Sunday for some time, eventually switching to meditating, spending time alone with nature, creating vision boards, writing down my goals and stating my desires to the Universe about having a healthy body, a happy spirit, a great career, etc. The Universe, divine energy, the primal cause or whatever you want to call it, was listening and it answered my prayers over the course of years by sending me the right books on nutrition, spirituality and different healing modalities. It listened by always providing me with the financial means to study and undergo cleanses in a number of holistic spas and institutes, by putting gifted healers and true spiritual teachers on my path at the right time.

If you do not know right now exactly how you are going to get out of your blues, you do not have to have the answers. God has the answers. God is the head honcho of all of creation and it is His job and joy to provide for us. All you have to do is to believe that the right solutions will come when the time is right. Perhaps the solution to your problems is the program that I am sharing here that saved my life. Whatever path of healing you choose, just have faith in universal intelligence that you will be taken care of. Faith makes the impossible possible. I know from my own personal experience that Naam Yoga and the Harmonyum Healing System are very powerful. Practiced to-gether or on their own they will guide you to the ultimate state of happiness. The thing is, as with all spiritual paths, you have to do your part, you have to have faith that your life is not hopeless and that there is a solution for your situation out there. Faith is the opposite of fear. When we have fear and focus on the negative, we can't help but see "evidence" that life is hard, that the world is not safe, and so we end up manifesting even more of the same. Our faulty beliefs become our concrete reality. Superior faith is knowing that something can be possible without having physical evidence of it. When you have 100% faith in something, whether it is healing from a disease, finding the love of your life, owning your own business and so on, one day it will manifest in your reality. In order for your desire to become your reality you must state your desire. Stating your desire for change is a huge part of getting there. The power of intention is an amazing force and when used properly and mixed with the sincere desire to be of service to others, it will bring miracles into your life. As I said, I used to write down my wishes to be happy, to stop binging, to stop picking my face and to stop drinking too much alcohol and coffee for years before they came true. They seemed impossible to achieve at the time of me writing them down, yet I kept hoping that one day everything would get better. I used to surround myself with images from magazines that created positive emotions inside of me. I then visualized them, feeling the emotions of happiness and excitement, like I had already achieved those goals. It could have taken me much less time to get my wishes, if I didn't resist so much and just allowed myself to be happy, but instead I was unwittingly sabotaging myself. So don't just ask for something, but also pay attention to whether you are really allowing what you want to manifest to come in and if you really have faith that what you are asking for is possible and is going to happen. Most dreams come true, if you ask for it and open yourself to the divine guidance. Trust in the process and have faith that you will get where you want to be at the right time. Know that anything you are going through is not a permanent situation. Never ever give up on yourself! We are all here on our own unique mission. No one else can replace you. One day, when you are done cleaning your mental and emotional garbage, and start feeling great about yourself, everything and everyone in your life, you will be a shining star of hope and faith to others, helping them through their dark times simply by being you.

I believe that faith in the Creator's love and ability to help us through any challenge is crucial in order to overcome it. It is the main reason why I feel happy and have a positive attitude more often than not, no matter what life is giving me. The next ingredient in this recipe, however, is faith in yourself. You must believe that you have what it takes to change your life for the better, no matter what circumstances you are dealing with right now. Even if you are feeling weak, lonely, poor or unlucky, you need to start thinking and feeling like a winner, and believing in yourself. I once heard that the most successful actors who make it in Hollywood are not the ones who possess the most talent, but who think that they possess the most talent. They are so confident in their ability to act that they convince everyone as well. Whether that is an absolute truth or not, it makes sense, as someone who is very talented but who thinks very little of himself/herself probably will not make it far at all.

Maybe you grew up in a family where you were never good enough or pretty enough for your parents. Maybe you have a romantic partner who constantly criticizes you. We do not have any way to control others and what they think of us. The only thing that you can control at any moment is your own opinion of yourself. Make the words you say to yourself as uplifting and positive as you can. Praise yourself for whatever you do well during the day, and even give yourself a hug every so often, it feels good! When you make a mistake, take a look at it constructively and then learn a lesson from it, without beating yourself up. Guess what? That is how everybody in this world learns. We are all making mistakes and correcting our course. I used to have all kinds of big hopes, wishes and dreams and very often the negative voice in my head would turn on and say, "Who do you think you are to ever do/have all those things? You are not good, pretty or smart enough to ever achieve them..." This went on for years and it would make me very depressed. One day I read that if you have a dream or an idea, it was given to you by God. God would never give you that vision, without providing you with the means of achieving it. Once I allowed this reality to sink into my consciousness, I realized that I want those things for very specific reasons, that they are in accordance with the Divine Plan, and I have everything I need within me to make them come true. Along with this new belief in myself and in my hopes came the right circumstances, the right people and the right tools to help me achieve my goals.

When you are humbly and sincerely self-confident, you will notice how much fun life becomes. You will finally be playing a lead role in your life as opposed to a set extra, and stars always get all of the glory and the biggest bucks! As the band "James" puts it in one of their songs, if others are not able to handle your bright light when you finally stop playing it safe and small, they can 'put their shades on'. Ask for everything you want and more and know that all things are possible. You are born to behappy and to shine bright!

Elena's Favorite Exercise to Replace Fear with Faith

Posture/Movement: Sit in Easy Pose with a straight spine and the chin slightly lowered. Bend the arms so that the hands are at shoulder level in Gyan Mudra (thumb touching the tip of the index finger) with the palms facing forward. Inhale through the nose with your hands in that position. As you exhale through the mouth, push the hands straight in front, parallel to the ground. Inhale through the nose as you bring the hands back to their starting position. Breathe deeply and continue to move back and forth with the arms at a moderately fast pace.

Focus: The eyes are slightly open and focused on the tip of the nose.

Breath: Inhale through the nose and exhale through the mouth while drawing the navel in.

Time: 3 minutes

To End: Inhale deeply, hold the breath, tighten every muscle in your body, and exhale. Inhale again and shake your wrists above your head. Exhale and relax the arms down.

18. Have fun and do what you love.

"Time you enjoy wasting, was not wasted." "Life is very short, and there's no time for fussing and fighting my friends." "Why in the world are we here? Surely not to live in pain and fear." ~ John Lennon

We all have a different idea of what fun is. Fun comes in many shapes and sizes. What is fun for one person is boring to someone else. Most of the time when we think about fun, it gets allocated to the weekends, going out with friends, having dinner with the family, going on a date, watching a movie or taking a drive somewhere far away. Since the majority of our lives are actually spent at work, I personally think that the major factor in having a constant blast is making a living by loving what you do. Doing what you love heals you and keeps you connected with your heart. If you do not love what you do, it zaps your energy and can lead to stress. People spend all day long making money and then they get sick. Evaluate what you think is important, what truly matters. Power, fame and how much money you have does not really matter if you are not happy. The real question to ask is, "Do I love what I do and do what I love?"

I used to think that I needed to become a successful career woman, have an amazingly fit body, a handsome husband with a great job, and two kids by the age of thirty. That is a lot of pressure! I set those goals for myself, unconsciously, in order to get my parents approval and to satisfy my ego! I wanted to have something to boast about to friends at dinner parties on Saturday night, and I felt that becoming a wife, an accomplished professional and eventually a mother would automatically qualify me as a "she made it" type. I devoted my entire twenties to reaching all of those goals and it landed me in the wrong relationship (which looked "perfect" on paper) and depressed. I had no clue what I wanted to have as a career. Furthermore, I was not "emotionally fit" to care for a child and felt like a total loser, who had let her parents and herself down. One beautiful day, I was struck with the realization that the only goal I should have was to be happy, to do what I love and to serve others. I realized that my choice of career needed to allow for those qualities, to be with people that I love, and most of all to have limitless fun loving and appreciating each day! I realized that it is not about what you do and how much money you make, or what position your husband holds, it is only about happiness. Happiness is all that matters. Life can and should be a total blast, a constant "dance party," and we all should be doing whatever gives us joy, pleasure and a sense of purpose, because these are the qualities that really make us happy. If your idea of fun is to travel the world, sleep on people's couches and make an occasional buck from a random job — I say do it! Even if your parents want you to be a doctor. On the other hand, if you cannot wait to be a doctor, and going to a hospital every day helping sick people is your idea of fun — do it! In any case, just decide to be true to yourself and get out of circumstances that make you miserable. Perhaps what would make you happy is to never work again, to find someone who loves taking care of you and in return you take care of that person, your home and your kids. If the idea of going to work every day doing a job that you can't stand, hating your life and trying to be someone you are not doesn't appeal to you anymore, then find what does! Maybe your idea of happiness is being totally self-reliant and stretching your limits to new horizons. There are no wrong answers. I learned through experience that with faith in the universe you will be always provided for and taken care of, and when you are having a good time doing what you love, you add to the vibration of goodness, love, peace and light in the world. This in itself is a form of service. Our world needs more love, peace and light and more happy, positive people.

If you are reading this right now and thinking that you have no idea what you would like to do that could make you happy, don't worry. The problem is not in not knowing. The real problem is in not knowing and never going through the effort to find out. The problem is when you are living your life on autopilot, doing something you hate just so you can pay bills, or because your title makes you feel important or it makes your parents happy. Don't let yourself become so miserable that you have to live vicariously through other people's experiences, through celebrities, or someone you may know who is having "an amazing, exciting life".

For a very long time I had no idea of what I wanted to do with my life. I ended up opening a business when I was 23 so that I could "make a lot of money as fast as possible and retire at 30". Needless to say I almost went bankrupt after a year, as "making lots of money" is not a healthy motivating force and certainly not a recipe for true success. I closed the business down and went through many part time jobs, a fitness position, vitamin sales, and a modeling career, all while searching for my purpose on Earth. Deep down I knew it needed to have something to do with helping people with their fitness and nutritional habits. So I kept praying and praying for the Universe to show me the signs, to give me an answer what I could do that would allow me to have a good life, be happy and of service to others, all at the same time. I used to do this exercise where you would close your eyes and think of what you would want to do with yourself, if you had all the money in the world. The answers would change a bit over the years, but they were all related. Eventually I learned what career makes me happy. It took me ten years of searching to finally figure it out. So if you are not one of those people I used to be jealous of, who knew what they are here to do from the day they were born, you still can and will find your true calling when the time is right, and when you start asking for the answer.

Elena's Million-Dollar Exercise

Find a space where you can be comfortable and uninterrupted. You may choose to play some relaxing music in the background. Sit comfortably with your spine straight, reaching to the sky through your crown chakra and bring your hands into Middle Pillar mudra which is formed by bringing the hands at the level of navel about six inches apart with the palms facing toward each other. Middle Pillar mudra is a powerful mudra that allows you to access your higher truth. Your left hand corresponds to love and the right hand to wisdom. It is a powerful mudra for healing. You can place yourself or a loved one (in your imagination) between your palms and send love and healing energy to that person.

While holding your hands in Middle Pillar mudra, breathe softly and gently through your nose. Close your eyes and ask your Higher Self to guide you toward answers that are in your highest good. Dare to imagine that you have all of the money that you could ever need. What would you do with your life? What career would you choose if money was the last thing on your mind? What would you do with your time and energy? Most successful people I know share that they would do exactly what they are already doing. Don't be afraid to let your mind soar, imagine that there are no obstacles between you and what you would love to do. Once you are clear on your vision, thank your higher self for guiding you. Now, it is up to you to make a plan to get there. You do not have to make drastic changes in your life. Just take one small step each day, one motion in the direction of your dreams.

19. Forgive yourself.

"The reality is that when you forgive, you are not doing it for the sake of the person who wounded you. You are rebuilding your heart and spirit to a state of grace. You are doing it to heal yourself. Forgiveness purifies and that purity makes you strong and radiant." ~ Dr. Joseph Michael Levry

I truly believe that each and every one of us is a shining star playing the leading role in this episode called life. Therefore, since you are a star, you need to think like a star. "Fake it till you make it," as they say. You need to model the consciousness of someone who is already living the life that you dream of. In Divine Spiritual Wisdom, we say, "What better star is there to learn from than the Sun?" Our beautiful amazing Sun is the perfect example of forgiveness. It shines its light upon everyone, good or bad, wealthy or poor, without discrimination or judgment. Saints and sinners alike are all fed and nourished by the Sun. Dr. Levry often refers to the Sun as, "A visible representation of the spirit of God in action." When we forgive others, we are becoming like the Sun, which extends its light to everyone, regardless if they are grateful and regardless if they may have done something that we didn't like.

One of my clients many years ago was sexually abused as a little girl. Her relatives did unspeakable things to her and now, as a woman, she relived these horrors in her mind everyday. She suffered from panic attacks, an eating disorder and had suicidal thoughts. What happened a long time ago was still thriving in her present day life. We were not able to continue our work together, as she was rigidly attached to being a victim and was full of hatred towards her family. Because she could only see herself as a victim, she had something happening to her almost every day: a dog would attack her, someone would push her in the street, or yell at her at work. I was not successful in helping her at that time, but I believe that if I had known some of the Naam Yoga techniques that I know now, I could have offered her a technology that could have accelerated her healing process. At that time however, she was not ready to let go of herself as she knew it — overweight, depressed, and a victim of abuse. I realized it was not my role to help her, and that no one could help her until she was ready to let go of the pain in her heart and to find her true joyful identity. I hope she is doing better today and send her my blessings. The point here is that sometimes we are attached to our suffering, labeling ourselves, "an eating disorder sufferer," or "abuse survivor," or "an addict", or "it's all my parents' fault, they made me this way." Those self-chosen labels become our constant companions and we even trick ourselves into thinking that they are our friends. I used to be one of those people who blamed my parents for everything that was wrong with me — my sugar addiction, my failures in relationships, my depression, my financial struggles, etc., until one day I realized that I just enjoyed being miserable and loved my sob stories. In reality, I have tremendously amazing parents. It is just that I had been choosing to focus on what I thought they did wrong for my entire life instead of what they did right. I saw the worst in them and blamed my shortcomings on them. When this realization washed over me, it took me literally less than a day to realize that all I needed to do was to see the best in them in order to arrive at my final destination of total forgiveness and acceptance. Nobody is perfect. That day, I decided to send my victim mentality into retirement and start being grateful for everything my parents had ever done for me, for doing their very best to give me and my brother a good life, and simply for the fact that they gave me a chance to experience this life by giving birth to me. That "hurt little girl" identity had to go if I wanted to shift into the happy life I had longed for so many years. I truly believe that the Naam meditations and the Harmonyum Healing sessions that I received regularly helped me to come to these conclusions. I was able to give my binge-eating label and my victim mentality a final burial. I had to let go of someone I used to think was "the real me" to get to the real me!

As I developed self-love and respect, as well as respect towards my parents, I lost my desire for sugar binging, and it's really not a big deal to me anymore. It feel wonderful and free to enjoy desserts when I do eat them simply because they taste good and not because I'm trying to overcompensate for a sense of lack. I kindly invite you to join me on this "freedom ride" and to start letting go of your past stories and self-identities that are no longer serving you, and to forgive everyone who did you wrong so that you can start living and enjoying your life. You have the choice to live an amazing life in the "here and now," and to become anyone you want to be, or remain stuck in the past, and therefore not really living and present for the beauty and abundance of joyful experiences that you are blessed with each day.

A great way to start the process of forgiveness is to decide that you are willing to let go of past hurts. You must forgive others and forgive yourself. Having the ability to forgive yourself is crucial, if you want to live the life of your highest potential and happiness. We all make mistakes and are not perfect, as we are all human. I found it was harder for me to forgive myself for my past wrongdoings than to forgive others. I was much harder on myself in my search for perfection than on anyone else. I realized that when I was able to accept myself fully with all of my past garbage and imperfections, that was when the true forgiveness of others could take place. You will never be able to become who you are supposed to be and find your true happiness until you get rid of your insecurities, shame and guilt. For that to happen you need to forgive yourself for mistakes that you have made in the past. Your past negative behavior and wrongdoings were based on your level of consciousness. Commit to working on yourself and raising your vibration. You need to forgive yourself for the wrongs you have done. Once you forgive yourself, it will be much easier for you to forgive others. Accept that we are all going to screw up along the way in some shape or form, as it is part of our learning process. It will make you a stronger, saner and ultimately a happier person.

Elena's Favorite Way to Forgive Yourself and Others

When I started my forgiveness journey, I used a lot of affirmations. They were very simple, yet I had to repeat them over and over for some time before they became my reality. I would say: "I fully accept and forgive myself." or "I accept and forgive so and so…" or "I am a good person and I love myself completely with all of my imperfections."

If you are feeling that you need some extra help with the process of forgiveness, try saying some of these affirmations or your own, as often as you need to, or write them down on a piece of paper and look at them once in a while when any feelings of guilt, anger or self-destruction creep in. I will share with you a yogic secret to make them even more powerful. Say the word "WAH!" in front of each affirmation while pulling the navel slightly in. "WAH" gives your affirmations power and strength. Saying "WAH!" before each affirmation makes it easier for change to happen on the physical plane.

CONCLUSION

I hope you enjoyed this book. I am so happy that you took time to learn how you can heal your emotional challenges naturally and in such a way that is guaranteed to bring you true happiness when applied on a regular basis. I hope we will stay in touch via social media and you can always check out my YouTube channel for video's on Happiness and Naam Yoga. I wish you so much success on your journey to becoming your True Self: Happy, unlimited, free from negative emotions and beliefs, prosperous and most positive you that you could ever imagine yourself being. We all want to change the world, and the fastest and the only true way to get there is by changing yourself first. It is my prayer that every morning when you wake up from now on, you will smile, and tell yourself, "I AM HAPPY!" Say it, feel it, BE IT.

Much Love, Peace and Light,

Elena

@elenavasilenka on Instagram and Twitter.

SOURCES

Connect with Elena and sign up for a Free video program on the techniques from this book : **www.elena.la**

Check out Elena's YouTube videos on Happiness and Naam Yoga:
www.youtube.com/channel/UCCTUxp6S7Ktl24rb--ZCBiQ

To order a "Naam Yoga Therapies for Happiness" DVD program: **www.elenavasilenka.com**

To learn more about Naam Yoga LA : **www.naamyoga.com**

To learn more about Dr. Levry's work, download Sacred Sound mantras, order his books or register for events with him around the world: **www.rootlight.com**

Elena Vasilenka

Made in the USA
San Bernardino, CA
20 September 2017